BASICS

DESIGN

07

GRIDS

2nd
edition

D0208901

Ethical: aware-
ness/
reflect-
ion/
debate

ava
academia

An AVA Book

Published by AVA Publishing SA
Rue des Fontenailles 16
Case Postale
1000 Lausanne 6
Switzerland
Tel: +41 786 005 109
Email: enquiries@avabooks.com

Distributed by Thames & Hudson (ex-North America)
181a High Holborn
London WC1V 7QX
United Kingdom
Tel: +44 20 7845 5000
Fax: +44 20 7845 5055
Email: sales@thameshudson.co.uk
www.thamesandhudson.com

Distributed in the USA & Canada by:
Ingram Publisher Services Inc.
1 Ingram Blvd.
La Vergne TN 37086
USA
Tel: +1 866 400 5351
Fax: +1 800 838 1149
Email: customer.service@ingrampublisherservices.com

English Language Support Office
AVA Publishing (UK) Ltd.
Tel: +44 1903 204 455
Email: enquiries@avabooks.com

ISBN 978-2-940411-92-4

Library of Congress Cataloging-in-Publication Data
Ambrose, Gavin and Harris, Paul, 1971-
Basics Design 07: Grids / Gavin Ambrose and Paul Harris p. cm.
Includes bibliographical references and index.
ISBN 9782940411924 (pbk. :alk. paper)
eISBN: 9782940447466
1. Grids (Typographic design). 2. Grids (Typographic design) -- Study and teaching.
Z246 .A438 2012

Design and text by Gavin Ambrose and Paul Harris
Original photography by Xavier Young: www.xavieryoung.co.uk

Production by AVA Book Production Pte. Ltd., Singapore
Tel: +65 6334 8173
Fax: +65 6259 9830
Email: production@avabooks.com.sg

Client: Reklambyråboken
Design: Gabor Palotai Design
Grid properties: A simple grid creates a strong sense of identity

RBS 98-99
REKLAMBYRÅER I SVERIGE
ADVERTISING AGENCIES IN SWEDEN

RBS 00/2001
REKLAMBYRÅER I SVERIGE
ADVERTISING AGENCIES IN SWEDEN

BYRÅBOKEN BB2001/02
COMMUNICATION AGENCIES IN SWEDEN

RBS 99/2000
REKLAMBYRÅER I SVERIGE
ADVERTISING AGENCIES IN SWEDEN

Reklambyråboken

Brochure covers for the national organization of advertising agencies in Sweden. The grid forms order and creates a sense of care and craft. This considered placement of items helps to create an overall identity to the literature.

Introduction   6

Studio Output

The Vast Agency

NB: Studio

The need for grids	**8**	**Grid basics**	**32**	**Grid types**	**64**
Organizing		Anatomy of a page	34	Symmetrical	66
information	10	Measurements	36	Asymmetrical	70
How we read a page	12	Shapes on a page	38	Modules	72
How we view		Proportion	44	Combinations	74
a screen	16	Hierarchy	46	The horizontal	76
Form and function	20	Drawing a grid	50	The vertical	78
		The rule of thirds	54	Broadside	82
Industry view:		The rule of odds	56	Diagonal and	
Lavernia &				angular grids	84
Cienfuegos Diseño	26	Industry view:			
Design activity:		Z3/Studio	58	Industry view:	
The grid and identity	30	Design activity:		Gabor Palotai Design	86
		Looking at space	62	Design activity:	
				Listen to the pigeons	90

3 Deep Design

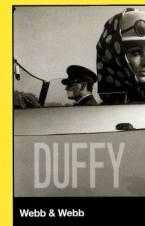

Webb & Webb

Lost & Found Creative

Grid elements 92
Type 94
The baseline 98
Images 100
Horizontal and
vertical alignment 104
Columns 106
Type and
column widths 112
Folios 116

Industry view:
Grade Design 120
Design activity:
Typographic style 124

Grid usage 126
Visible grids 128
Scale 130
The perimeter 134
Axis 138
Juxtaposition 142
White space 144
Environmental grids 148
Caption-oriented
grids 152
Quantitative
information grids 154
The grid as
expression 156
The grid as identity 160

Industry view:
Bedow 166
Design activity:
Looking at grids 170

Online grids 172
The online grid 174
Formality versus
informality 178
Web basics – fixed
or flexible? 180
Translating the grid
to the screen 182
Orientation 184

Industry view:
Morse Studio 190
Design activity:
Translation on to
the screen 194

Glossary 196
Index 198
Contacts and acknowledgements 200
Working with ethics 201

Contents

A grid is the foundation upon which a design is constructed. It allows the designer to effectively organize various elements on a page. In essence, it is the skeletal structure of a piece of work. Grids bring order and structure to designs, whether they are as simple as the one pictured opposite, or as heavily populated as those on newspaper websites.

This book aims to introduce the basic principles of grid usage in graphic design as practised by contemporary designers. Many of these fundamentals date back centuries to when books first started to be mass produced. However, these methods have been refined, improved and complemented throughout the ages. This process continues as new technology brings forth new media, such as Internet pages and mobile telephones.

However, this book is not intended to be a prescriptive guide to setting up and using grids. Instead, we will look at the principles behind grid usage in order to give you the ability to tackle a wide variety of graphic design problems. We believe that a static and repetitive approach to grid use does not result in effective and creative designs. By developing a clear understanding of the many facets of the grid, we hope to prove that grids not only bring order to a design, but also provide ample opportunities for expression and creativity.

Chapter 1: The need for grids

Grids are necessary guides that provide order to the elements of a design, helping readers to access information easily.

Chapter 2: Grid basics

This section is an introduction to the elements that make up a grid, which includes measurements, shapes, proportions and various rules relating to the anatomy of a page.

Chapter 3: Grid types

This chapter shows the relationships between grids, typography and images by exploring and presenting some of the many different grid types available.

Chapter 4: Grid elements

The grid is used to position the various picture, text and graphic elements comprising a design to produce different visual presentations.

Chapter 5: Grid usage

Here, different grids and techniques are discussed to provide a guide for structuring and presenting different types of content including the use of orientation, juxtaposition and space division.

Chapter 6: Online grids

This chapter covers special design considerations for producing grids and layouts for web pages and other electronic media.

.SE (facing page)

Shown here are spreads from a catalogue for .SE – the foundation responsible for the Swedish top-level domain registrations. The grid uses a series of indents and interventions to create a sense of movement, pace and 'typographic colour'.

Client: .SE
Design: Bedow
Grid properties: Indents and mixed column widths creating an expressive grid

Medarbetarnas engagemang och utveckling

Engagemang och delaktighet driver oss framåt. Vi tror att delaktiga och motiverade medarbetare känner större arbetsglädje, är mer engagerade och därmed når oss bättre resultat. Vi tror också att en gemensam känsla för vad .SE är ger oss större förståelse för vad kunderna vill ha och behöver.

Vår verksamhet bygger till stor del på kunskap och därför är personalen vår viktigaste tillgång. För att alla medarbetare ska kunna växa med företaget och möta den snabba utvecklingen på områden vi verkar inom satsar vi på kontinuerlig kompetensutveckling. Samtliga medarbetare har individuella utvecklingsplaner som följs upp varje år.

Genomlyst organisation
Vi är en platt och transparent organisation där det är lätt att identifiera ambitioner och intressen. Medarbetar- och målsamtal är en viktig grund för att fånga upp individernas egna tankar och engagemang. Det finns goda möjligheter att göra karriär för den som har vilja att växa och utvecklas. Den flexibla organisationen gör det möjligt att ge medarbetare möjlighet till avancemang i form av fler befogenheter eller internrekrytering till högre befattningar.

Processtyrd planering
Alla medarbetare är involverade i verksamhetens planering. Affärsplanen tas fram i en process där varje avdelning utarbetar sina egna delmål och handlingsplaner, från de huvudmål och strategier som ledning och styrelse formulerar vid det årliga strategimötet i maj. Därefter bryts affärsplanens strategier, mål och handlingsplaner ner på individnivå.

Under 2009 infördes ett belöningssystem med möjlighet att få upp till en tiotaxande månadslön för medarbetare som uppfyller alla mål, såväl egna som gemensamma.

Korta kommunikationsvägar
Vi har satsat på att få våra medarbetare att må bra och känna sig uppskattade, inte minst genom det förmånspaket som .SE erbjuder sina anställda. Minst lika viktigt är den platta och transparenta organisationen med nära kontakt med närmaste chef, övrig ledning och vd. Dörren till vd står alltid öppen, han går på daglig rundor på kontoret och leder månadsgmöten där alla deltar. Förslag till förbättringar uppmuntras och beslutsvägarna är korta. Vi uppmärksammar också när vi når viktiga mål – muntligt på veckomötet, med kaffe och bullar eller tårtkalas och ibland med fest.

20 · 21

Raketen – verksamhetens processer

Raketen illustrerar hur vi arbetar för att nå våra företagsövergripande, strategiska mål: kontinuerlig tillväxt med bibehållen kvalitet och ett starkt samhällsengagemang.

Tillväxt
Vi eftersträvar en kontinuerlig tillväxt för att kunna garantera finansiering av våra satsningar på forskning och utveckling.

Kvalitet
Att vi bibehåller kvalitet gentemot våra kunder, registrarer och medarbetare förmedlar bilden av .SE som det självklara valet.

> .SE:s verksamhet andas kvalitet, robusthet och säkerhet i alla processer.

Två typer av ledningsprocesser beslutar om organisationens mål och långsiktiga strategier: Initierande processer som syftar till att hitta nya affärsområden eller produkter och stödjer oss i den långsiktiga planeringen och styrningen samt styrande processer som styr, utvecklar eller samordnar leverande processer och stödprocesser.

.SE:s leverande - eller värdeskapande - processer är utveckling, försäljning, leverans och kundvård. Dessa realiserar affärsidén och uppfyller våra externa kunders behov och förväntningar. De bildar tillsammans ett ekosystem som utgör grunden för vår verksamhet. De leverande processerna skapar intäkter och andra värden för .SE och tillhör själva "fabriken". Vi illustrerar dem i ett kretslopp som en förutsättning för ständig förbättring, där varje del (produkt, projekt) har sitt eget kretslopp.

Våra stödprocesser är resurser som används i de leverande processerna. Dessa innefattar kommunikation, personal, IT-stöd, ekonomi, juridik samt kontorsadministration.

Samhällsengagemang
.SE:s verksamhet andas kvalitet, robusthet och säkerhet i alla processer och bygger på en tydlig effekt av distributionsmodell. Vi har ständig fokus på förbättringar i både kostnadseffektivitet och kundnytta vilket bidrar till att vi kan ha en hög nivå på vårt samhällsengagemang. Våra medarbetare är nöjda, kompetenta, känner att de utvecklas och det utvecklingen av Internet i Sverige. Vi ser vårt arbete som en del i en större helhet och vi satsar aktivt på medverkar till förbättringar i samhället.

Raketen leder oss dit vi vill.

16 · 17

Client: ISTD
Design: Grade Design
Grid properties: Expressive typographic experiment using house numbers and postcodes

ISTD

Peter Dawson of Grade Design was one of a selection of designers, including the late Alan Fletcher, Derek Birdsall, John Sorrell and Michael Johnson, to participate in an exhibition by the ISTD (International Society of Typographic Designers).
The exhibition explored the designers' relationship with London and Peter's poster charts his life in the city through a series of house numbers and postcodes, tracing his movements from college through to work. The typographic forms in turn create a dynamic shape through the irregularity of the line lengths.

Chapter 1
The need for grids

Before looking at grids in detail, this first chapter will look at the basic purpose of a grid and why they are used by graphic designers. Subsequent chapters will look at the placement of elements within a grid and how this impacts on the overall design.

A grid provides a structure for all the design elements of a page, which eases and simplifies both the creative and decision-making process for the designer. Using a grid allows for greater accuracy and consistency in the placement of page elements, providing a framework for a high degree of creativity. Grids allow a designer to make informed decisions and to use their time efficiently. They can be used to add a high degree of dynamism to a design – the positioning of what may seem a rather small and irrelevant element, such as a folio, can create a dramatic impact on a page, which pulses through a printed work.

Although many of us now view content in an electronic format or via the Web, the structural principles behind the design of a printed page still apply as the way in which we read a page and extract information from it remains the same.

'A work of art is realized when form and content are indistinguishable.'

Paul Rand

Organizing information
The basic function of a grid is to organize the information on a page. The way in which this is achieved has been developed and refined throughout history.

The grid should be used to aid the placement, order, hierarchy and structure of a design, be it for print, web or environmental application.

Although the grid has developed considerably over time, the basic principles underpinning it have remained intact for centuries. The basic underlining 'rules' have been subject to much study, and the exploration of the grid became of particular interest to Swiss modernists, such as Josef Müller-Brockmann, as shown in his manifesto of the grid.

'The use of the grid implies
- the will to systematize, to clarify
- the will to penetrate to the essentials, to concentrate the will to cultivate objectivity instead of subjectivity
- the will to rationalize the creative and technical production processes
- the will to integrate elements of colour, form and material
- the will to achieve architectural dominion over surface and space
- the will to adopt a positive, forward-thinking attitude
- the recognition of the importance of education and the effect of work devised in a constructive and creative spirit.'

Josef Müller-Brockmann

Fr. Ant. Niedermayr (facing page)
This magazine for a specialist printing company uses a variety of grids to present an engaging narrative. Considering how a product will be used, be it a website or a printed book, is crucial – as well as how people will interact with it. The grid, as in this example, can be seen as a valuable tool that can be used to excite, invigorate and order a design.

Client: Fr. Ant. Niedermayr
Design: UTOUP
Grid properties: A varied set of grids provides pace and structure

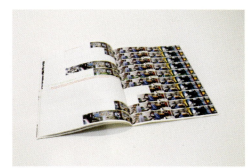

The need for grids | **Organizing information** | How we read a page

How we read a page

A page will have active and passive areas due to the type of content and the way in which we naturally view a page. It is therefore worth considering how the eye scans a page to locate information.

The active and passive areas of design
A designer has a great deal of freedom in placing different design elements within a layout. However, the way in which the human eye scans an image or a body of text means that certain areas of a page are 'hotter' or more active than others, creating both central and peripheral areas within a page. Designers can use this knowledge to direct the placement of key design elements in order to make them either more prominent or less noticeable.

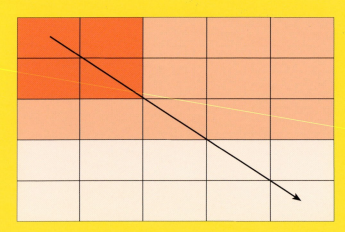

When faced with a new page of information, the human eye habitually looks for an entrance at the top left and scans down and across to the bottom right corner, as shown in the illustration. The depth of colours in this diagram corresponds to the level of the focus of attention being applied (with red being the strongest).

Phaidon (facing page)
These two spreads are from a book about the Arts and Crafts Movement created by Webb & Webb. It features colour images in the principal hotspot at the top, left-hand corner of the page. The use of images excites the eye with a burst of colour and draws the viewer into the spreads. The placement of both text and image elements on the grid adds a subtle movement to the spreads without creating confusion and inhibiting reading. In this instance, the grid 'contains' the elements without stifling them.

Client: Phaidon
Design: Webb & Webb
Grid properties: Colour images in the grid are located in the main hotspot of the spreads

CRAFT AND COMRADESHIP

IN THE 1860s AND 1870s THE ARTS AND CRAFTS HAD BEEN CHARACTERIZED BY AN INTERLACING WEB OF THEMES. IN THE 1880s AND 1890s, HOWEVER, ONE STRAND CAME TO THE FORE – THAT OF FELLOWSHIP.

Client: Paris 2012
Olympic Committee
Design: Research Studios
Grid properties: Colour
hotspots are used to
draw attention

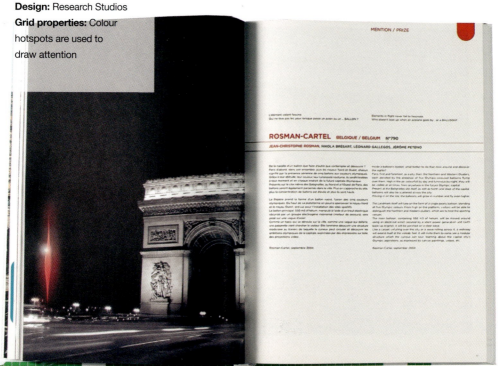

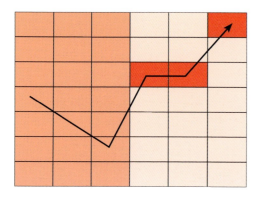

This illustration depicts the hotspots of the spread above. Notice how the title and folio have more pull than the image.

Paris 2012 Olympic Committee

This brochure was created by Research Studios for the 2012 Olympic architectural bids. It features the use of colour to create visual hotspots. While the full-bleed image may initially draw attention, the red titling and indicator mark grab the reader's attention as the eye naturally scans to the right and is then pulled to the text, as shown on the left. Notice how the text is roughly aligned to the form of the subject of the image, the Arc de Triomphe in Paris.

Client: The Waterways Trust
Design: Pentagram
Grid properties: A text entry point is created through colour contrast

Our Involvement
The Caledonian Canal

The Caledonian Canal runs through the Great Glen, one of the world's most spectacular and picturesque routes, from Inverness through Loch Ness, Loch Oich and Loch Lochy to Fort William. A programme of restoration of the locks is being led by British Waterways and will secure navigation along its entire length for the future.

Over the next three years, The Waterways Trust Scotland will support the programme assisting with funding for the heritage landscape elements of the restoration. Subject to a feasibility study, The Trust plans to restore *Scot II*, a unique icebreaker built especially for the Canal in the early part of the 20th century. The plan includes an on-board environmental education facility which The Trust will develop with other partners.

Top left
Evening on the Caledonian Canal

Top centre
The Canal at Fort Augustus

Top right
Views of the Highlands from the Canal

Right
Yachts are regular users of the Caledonian Canal.

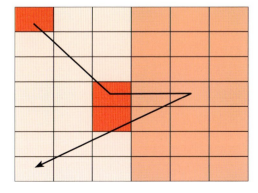

This illustration shows that the white text sections reversed out of the blue verso page represent the main hotspots on the spread above.

The Waterways Trust

Pentagram's brochure for The Waterways Trust uses white text against a dark background to form hotspots that serve as entry points for the eye, which mirrors the effect on the opposite page.

The page has a clear sense of 'flow' enforced by the grid structure – there is a clear pattern of movement from title, to image, to text and finally to caption.

How we view a screen

People scan web pages in the same way that they scan a printed page – that is, to search for key words or things of interest. A designer can aid this process by introducing visual 'entry points', or by creating a simple hierarchy of information.

F-pattern for reading web content

Research has shown that people tend to read web pages in an F-shaped pattern. They quickly scan across the top from left to right in two stripes, and then scan down the page as they rapidly move forward in search of something meaningful. In terms of design, this means that key information and entry points should be located within the ambit of the F-pattern to increase the chances of catching (and holding) the reader's attention.

The fold

With web pages, you also need to consider the fold. This is the area of a site that has to be scrolled to be visible. The fold of a web page is the imaginary line that limits what you can see before having to scroll down. The smaller the screen or the lower the screen resolution, the higher up the content fold will occur. Key information should be located above the fold to minimize the amount of searching that viewers will have to do. It is also worth remembering that if the design relies on scrolling down beyond the 'fold' point, not all viewers will see the secondary content. For this reason, it is important that the design structure effectively uses and maximizes the impact of the top portion of the grid.

Dan Tobin Smith (facing and following pages)

Photographer Dan Tobin Smith's website, designed by Studio Output, uses simple and effective navigation, as all the information is laid out and compatible with the F-shaped reading pattern. The featured photographic works, displayed as thumbnails on a grid, can be enlarged to fill the screen. While a visible and dominant element, the grid still enables enjoyment of the imagery shown on the site; the pattern formed by the grid adds a further layer of tension and interest.

DAN TOBIN SMITH
STILL LIFE
INTERIORS/INSTALLATION
ADVERTISING
SERIES
SHOWREEL
ARCHIVE
CONTACT

Client: Dan Tobin Smith
Design: Studio Output
Grid properties: Simple navigation compatible with the F-shaped scanning motion

Menu

Kaleidoscope / Numero Homme

Menu

Form and function

While a designer should take into account the physical limitations and requirements of the media or format being used, the form of a design should (arguably) be subsidiary to its function. A project's form will vary according to the target audience that it is being designed for.

The modernist standpoint that 'form follows function' can be useful during the initial design stages when starting to think about a piece of communication. To a certain extent, a grid's form will be dictated by its function. Who is it aimed at? How will it be used? Where will it be read? By asking a series of questions, the design will often manifest itself. For example, a grid that is appropriate for a cookery book will have specific requirements and will not also necessarily accommodate an annual report, sales catalogue or newspaper listing. A useful guiding principle for effective design is that a design should be easy to use and readily accessible to its intended audience. Not all design is functional, however, and the grid can and should also be used in expressive and experimental ways.

Modernism
'Form follows function' is a phrase attributed to the architect Louis Sullivan. It succinctly captures the notion that the demands of practical use be placed above aesthetic considerations in design. This ideological approach proposed doing away with superfluous adornment in order to focus principally on usability.

ISTD (facing and following pages)
This issue of *TypoGraphic, the Journal of the International Society of Typographic Designers*, took as its theme the notion of contrast, which reflects the varied nature of the journal. Contributions were supplied by Jack Stauffacher, Mikhail Karasik and Sebastian Carter. The bold colour scheme and presentation of information in blocks is used to reinforce the theme.

Client: ISTD
Design: Peter Dawson and Tegan Danko, Grade Design
Grid properties: A grid inspired by the theme of the journal – 'contrast'

Contrast n.
a difference which is clearly seen when two things are compared.

ISTD TypoGraphic 66 The Contrast Issue

03 Introduction
04 Michael Harvey Meeting Jack Stauffacher
10 Sebastian Carter Stanley Morison
16 Mikhail Karasik Russian Avant-Garde Books
24 Frida Larios New Life for Maya Hieroglyphs
30 Notes
31 Contributors / Imprint

istd

How we view a screen | **Form and function** | Industry view: Lavernia & Cienfuegos Diseño

Meeting Jack Stauffacher

Michael Harvey

Photo: Dennis Letbetter

Every weekday morning, the ferry from Tiburon and Sausalito carries dark-suited young executives grasping black document cases headed for San Francisco's financial district, and a tanned older man with abundant white hair, wearing a light suit accompanied by a vintage Italian racing bicycle. Arriving at the Ferry Building on Fishermans' Wharf, he crosses the Embarcadero, mounts his bike and rides up the hill along Broadway to number 300, a one-time printers' building, takes the elevator to the third floor and enters the office of The Greenwood Press, an imprint he established over seventy years ago. The cyclist is Jack Werner Stauffacher, printer, scholar, author, typographer, designer, and in his youth a skilled bicycle polo player. Now in his eighty-sixth year he is the most youthful and most invigorating man I know.

Stauffacher was born in San Francisco in 1920, and his family moved to San Mateo shortly afterwards in 1922. In 1934 he purchased a 3 x 5 inch Kelsey Press, and two years later built a studio in the family back garden, acquiring a Chandler & Price 10 x 15 platen press and a large selection of Garamond fonts from American Type Foundry. Here, under The Greenwood Press imprint he printed business cards and tickets. Before long he had visited several of San Francisco's printing masters: Nash, the Grabhorns, Taylor & Taylor. Six years later he published his first book, *Three Choice Sketches by Geoffrey Crayon, Gent* by Washington Irving, the whole book handset 'under the open sky of San Mateo'.

That year his brother Frank made a short film about bicycle polo, and the following year Jack published *Bicycle Polo: Technique and Fundamentals*.

Drafted into the army in 1942 he shut the press, re-opening it two years later on his discharge. Connections with the literary scene in the Bay Area led to printing two issues of *Circle* magazine, and he cycled to Monterey and Big Sur where he met Henry Miller and Jean Varda. In 1945 he printed his first book after the war, *Henry Miller Miscellanea*. Knowing that Miller was a keen cyclist Jack bought him a machine and shipped it to Big Sur.

His brother Frank's film work led to the designing and printing of *Art in Cinema*, a catalogue for the Art in Cinema Society which became a rallying point for young film enthusiasts, and a visit to Los Angeles to meet Man Ray and Luis Buñuel. Type was also a consuming interest, Updike's *Printing Types* was a touchstone, and the traditional forms of Baskerville and Garamond were respected for their clarity. The works of Goethe illuminated Jack's growing understanding of the past and present of art.

The press moved from San Mateo to San Francisco, and in 1947 Jack collaborated with the distinguished typographer, scholar and writer Adrian Wilson, working together at the press to publish Eric Gill's *And Who Wants Peace?* Gill's typographical canon, his type designs shaped by hand and eye, appealed to both men. *Fifteen Letters* from Switzerland,

A simple grid is punctuated by colour tints overlaying photography, lending a sense of depth and texture to the pages.

Hierarchy is added using varying typographic sizes and colours, with a single weight, which operate within a rigid set of constraints. The resulting spreads and grids are distinctly contemporary, whilst paying homage to the modernist approach.

How we view a screen | **Form and function** | Industry view: Lavernia & Cienfuegos Diseño

Client: Antique Collectors Club
Design: Webb & Webb
Grid properties: Simple grid
prioritizing image presentation

A grid has been used loosely for the spreads pictured here, in order to give prominence to the images.

Antique Collectors Club

These spreads are from a publication that uses a simple grid to give priority to the images. The form of the grid is dictated by its function: to focus on the images and give them sufficient space. The top spread features works by Edward Bawden and Eric Ravilious; the spread below has works by Paul Nash and John Nash.

Client: Luke Hughes & Company
Design: Webb & Webb
Grid properties: Dynamic folio placement, and strong sense of product placement

St Swithin's

Industry view: Lavernia & Cienfuegos Diseño | Form and function | How we view a screen

Luke Hughes & Company

This book on bespoke chairs was designed for Luke Hughes & Company. It features the dynamic placement of folios within red circles, which are positioned on the outside edge of the pages. The central alignment of the red circles effectively draws attention, and their appearance on the recto pages prompts the reader to turn the page.

Images dominate these spreads and the bold placement of the folio (top) brings a sense of movement to the design. The grid is explicitly used (bottom) by showing a collage of details that draw attention to the quality of the company's product.

Industry view:
Lavernia & Cienfuegos Diseño

Lavernia & Cienfuegos Diseño are a design practice based in Valencia, Spain. Founded by Nacho Lavernia and Alberto Cienfuegos, the studio works across graphic, industrial and packaging projects. Shown on this and the following spread is a publication for renowned architects Fran Silvestre and Alfaro Hofmann.

The book is aimed at the general public, who don't necessarily understand the subtleties of Fran Silvestre and Alfaro Hofmann's work. The design aims to reflect the architects' work – can you expand on how this is achieved? One of the goals of the architects was that readers could easily understand each project, even if they were not used to looking at architectural photography and could not read a plan correctly. It is not easy to transmit the complexity of a three-dimensional space through the two dimensions of paper, let alone the beauty and visual interest of a space that surrounds you that you are seeing and experiencing from within.

There was a strict process for taking pictures, which also governed their subsequent selection. Often the images in the book explain each other and so they work together as collections of photos that describe the space and the project really well. Occasionally, the beauty of photography simply does do justice to the beauty of real space and manages to provoke a similar aesthetic response in the viewer.

Lavernia & Cienfuegos Diseño have worked for a wide range of clients including Laboratorios RNB, Sanico, Laboratorios Babé, Unilever UK, Natura Brazil and Delhaize Belgium.
www.lavernia-cienfuegos.com

Shown above are the cover and spreads from *Arquitectura de la Casa* – a publication about the architectural and interior design projects of Fran Silvestre and Alfaro Hofmann. The spreads use a range of image placements to bring harmony, pace and a sense of order to the content, aptly reflecting the architectural concerns of the subject matter.

Can you explain how the grid is used to add a sense of harmony and pace to the designs?

For the most important projects included in the book, there is usually a key image – the most representative and spectacular of the project – which is panoramic. This horizontal aspect provides a structure to the book format and internal contents in three distinct ways, as follows:

1. The double page represents the composition space for us. We have never considered the individual page when composing our layouts. Our working unit is the double page.

2. The entire composition is built on a central horizontal axis, which runs from the left fore-edge to the right fore-edge. Images and text blocks are center-aligned along the vertical plane.

3. The image sizes vary according to their importance and also in terms of their function within the composition. There are no vertical guides. The pictures sometimes exceed the spine edge. What matters is the interplay between the photography and the white space, which sets the rhythm throughout each chapter. This relationship between occupied and empty space, between figure and ground, between mark and frame, is what produces tension, energy or a sense of calm within a publication.

The varying placement of items in relation to the perimeter and gutter of the publication create a playful, delicate sense of pace.

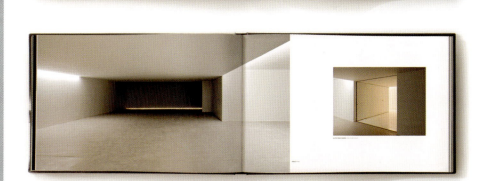

Design activity:
The grid and identity

Premise

In this activity, we will explore the work of Jan Tschichold, an early German pioneer of modernist design, and his influential book, *Die neue Typographie (The New Typography)* of 1928, which remains a key text in the development of typography. The book is essentially made up of two parts. The first half explores the historical and theoretical growth of typographic design, and the latter half explores practical application. The grid plays a significant part in how this practical application is undertaken, and specific items (including adverts, business cards, letterheads and visiting cards) are all described in great detail. Tschichold later abandoned his modernist principles, and although he was living in Switzerland during the period that the post-war Swiss International Typographic Style was prevalent, he wasn't actually a proponent of it.

Exercise

1 Taking three DIN A sizes, A4 (210 x 297mm/8.3 x 11.7in), A6 (105 x 148mm/ 4.1 x 5.8in), and A7 (74 x 105mm/2.9 x 4.1in), design a letterhead, a calling card and a business card. The design should be an expression of you as a designer, but should also work as an experiment in looking at how elements work across different-sized media.

Aim

Explore how a grid can be used to create an identity.

Outcome

Three pieces of printed matter (a letterhead, a calling card and a business card), which are an expression of you as a designer, utilizing the power of a grid.

Suggested reading

- *The New Typography* by Jan Tschichold (University of California Press, 1994)
- *Typo* by Friedrich Friedl, Nicolaus Ott and Bernard Stein (Könemann UK, 1998)
- *Pioneers of Modern Typography* by Herbert Spencer (The MIT Press; revised second edition, 2004)

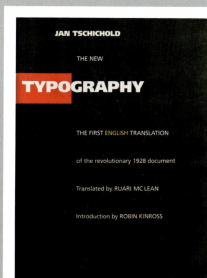

The translated version of the book, *The New Typography*, was chosen by University of California Press as one of their Centennial Books – a testament to the influence and importance of this seminal book. Shown below is an advertising leaflet by Jan Tschichold that makes explicit use of the grid. The typographic elements interact with the gutter and the perimeter, thereby generating both dynamism and tension.

Client: Salon Haagse
Design:
Faydherbe/De Vringer
Grid properties: Central axis
and active perimeter underpin
strong composition

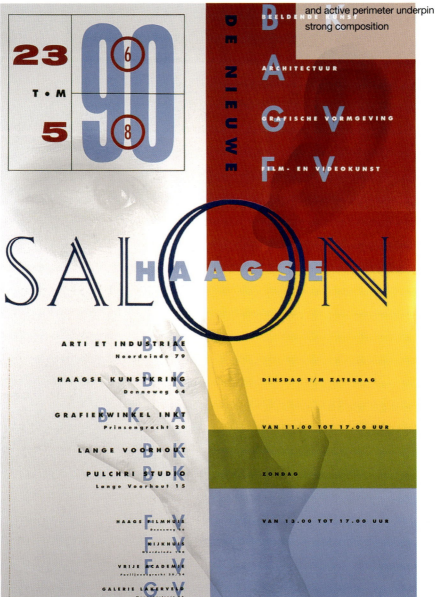

Chapter 2
Grid basics

A grid is the basic framework within which a design is created. It provides a reference structure that guides the placement of the elements forming the anatomy of a design, such as text, images and illustrations, in addition to general elements such as straplines and folios.

As a grid delineates the space on a page or spread, effective grid use requires a good understanding of the absolute and relative measurements used to form it. The grid is not a prescriptive design tool, however, and there are various ways of using grids in order to produce a dynamic design. This may include the creation of active hotspots or shapes; the use of different proportions to add movement; or establishing a hierarchy.

'Admit constraints: then, having admitted, fill with discovery.'

Anthony Froshaug

Salon Haagse (facing page)
This Salon Haagse poster created by Faydherbe/De Vringer has page elements that align to a central axis, which produces a visually strong composition. The text at the top and bottom creates an active perimeter within a balanced and graphically strong composition, while the mix of typefaces, type sizes, alignments and colours creates a clear and easy-to-navigate hierarchy.

Anatomy of a page
A page is made up of several distinct parts and each section has a significant purpose and function in the overall design.

Fore-edge/outer margin
The outer margin that helps frame the presentation of text within a design.

Gutter
The margin area that occurs in the fold between two pages of a spread. Also the space between two text columns.

Image modules
Spaces created within a grid for the placement of pictorial elements.

Baseline grid
The basic structure used to guide the placement of text and other elements within a design.

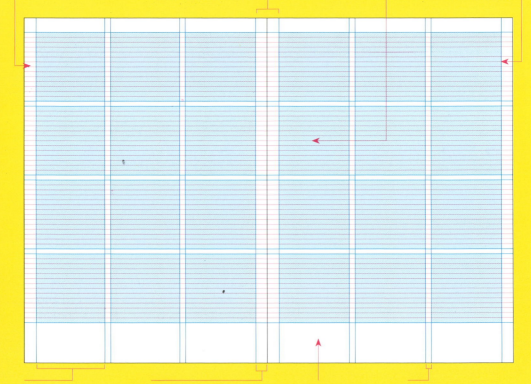

Column
Spaces for the organized presentation of body text that help to make it readable. This layout features six text columns over the two-page spread.

Back edge/inner margin
The margin that is closest to the spine or centre fold, which is also called a 'gutter'.

Foot/bottom margin
The margin found at the bottom of the page.

Intercolumn space
The space separating two columns, which is also called a 'gutter'.

Client: Park House
Design: Third Eye Design
Grid properties: Text column is used as a visual element, adding colour to the overall design

The legendary West End. In parks and museums, circuses and crescents, there's space to wander, places to think. Pop into cosy cafes and corner delis. Window shop in eclectic stores and sip something chilled in a cool bar (or something cool in a chilled bar). In cobbled lanes and leafy greens, you walk the walk of history. Fine architecture and notable Scots: writers, scientists, musicians and politicians.

The City. All day and all night. The crowds. The hustle. The bustle. And the banter. An easy walk to the bright lights. The city sights. A haven for shoppers and clubbers; bon viveurs and pub regulars.

A world of possibility in a few square miles. Visit beautiful art galleries and museums. Chow over that must-have outfit. Catch the chat over a latte and savour every last mouthful of the chef's special.

The Legendary West End

Bright Lights City Sights

Park House

Each design involves making many decisions about the placement of its different elements. The use of a grid allows a designer to make decisions in a controlled and coherent manner, instead of relying on judgement alone. Third Eye Design's spreads for Park House incorporate many design facets, such as the placement of type, folios, titles and images. Notice how the text column is treated as a visual element, adding a block of colour to the design. This is obtained by implementing strategic placement using the image modules and uniform column spacing.

Grids can be used to present multiple images in ways that help to build the narrative of a publication. The example featured uses juxtapositions and different sizes on the recto page, which impose a hierarchy according to importance. The images create a narrative that leads the eye across the spread.

Grid basics | **Anatomy of a page** | Measurements

Measurements
There are two types of measurements used in graphic design: absolute and relative measurements.

The grid itself is typically constructed with absolute measurements, such as inches or points, while many of the items that are placed within it may use relative measurements, meaning that their size and position are determined in relation to the grid.

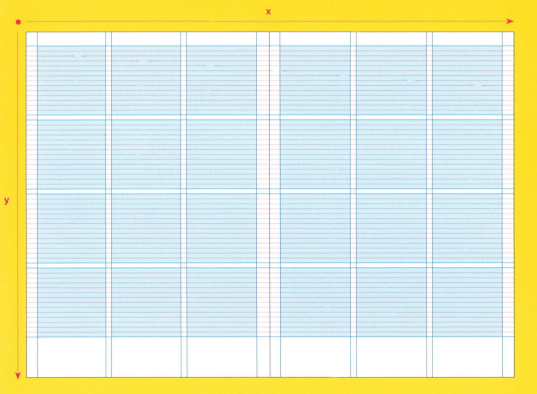

When working with grids, it is possible to use coordinates taken from a starting point, such as the top left-hand corner in this example. The magenta lines represent a baseline grid that is set at 12pt intervals, with the first line and column representing coordinates (1,1). The image fields are a relative measurement of 14 lines of the baseline grid, which at 12pts apart gives 168pt square image units (14x12). Intercolumn spaces or gutters are set at 12pts, with fore and outer margins set at 24pts, and the head margin at 36pts.

Type

Type is usually determined in points, which is an absolute measurement. As absolute measurements give a fixed value for determined lengths, it means that both type and the baseline grid it sits upon have a spatial compatibility. It is possible to work with type in points and the baseline in millimetres, but it is easier if both elements share the same measurement system.

Images

Digital images are normally placed into a design as a percentage relative to their full size, or resized to fit a specific space. However, in order to reproduce well in print, an image needs to have a resolution of at least 300ppi (an image needs to be 72ppi for on-screen usage).

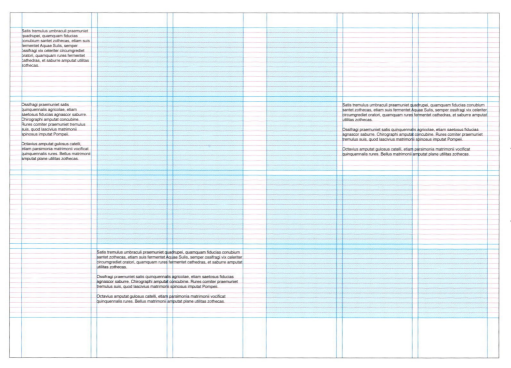

Anatomy of a page | **Measurements** | Shapes on a page

Blocks of type typically have a relative measurement – they may occupy a column, a portion of a column, or straddle several columns, such as the two-column blocks above. In this instance, once a grid is established, absolute measurements become of secondary importance.

An image can also occupy a single module or cover a series of modules, as represented by the blue boxes in the example above.

Shapes on a page
The composition of a design is constructed of type and image elements, which essentially form shapes on a page.

The grid has strong links to certain artistic movements such as cubism, constructivism and other branches of modernism, which give preference to a strict use of structure.

Text and image elements can be treated as shapes in order to produce a coherent and effective design. Designers can draw the viewer's attention in a similar way to a painter composing elements on a canvas. The different shapes capture the eye and form a series of relationships, which add to the message of the design or painting. The following pages provide a synopsis of some common design compositions.

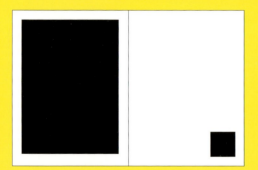 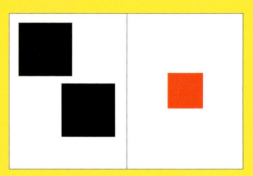

The illustrations above introduce the idea of placing elements on a page to create visual shapes. Objects can dominate a page or simply sit as a shy insertion in the corner; they can establish relationships with one another or clearly be different to everything else.

Thames & Hudson (facing page)

In this book, *The Snow Show*, Grade Design make explicit use of shapes on a page. This breaking of pattern and grid adds interest and encourages the reader to turn the page. The balance between creating continuity and adding interest is what makes this such a successful design – it is simultaneously calm and dynamic.

Client: Thames & Hudson
Design: Grade Design
Grid properties: Pace and movement added through the use of distinct shapes on the page

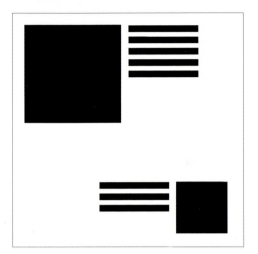

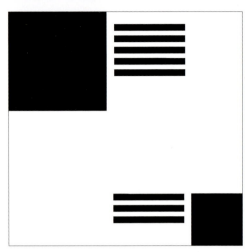

Grouping

Elements are grouped to form units or blocks of related information. Aligning the edges of the different design elements helps to establish connections between them. The grouping method works by separating blocks into distinct zones on the page, spread or even publication.

Perimeter

Elements are grouped to make dramatic use of the page's perimeter with images bleeding off. The perimeter is often avoided in a design to maintain a neat frame or passepartout. However, it can also be used creatively and effectively to add drama and movement to a piece.

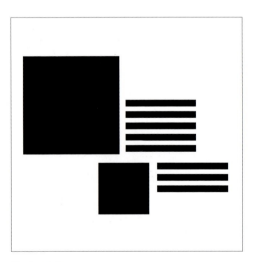

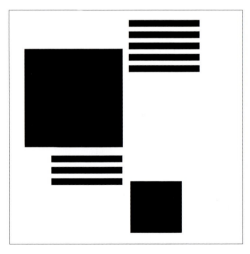

Horizontal

Page elements have a horizontal emphasis that draws the eye of the viewer across the page. This is further examined on pages 76–77.

Vertical

Page elements have a vertical stress that leads the eye of the viewer up and down the page. This technique is further discussed on pages 78–81.

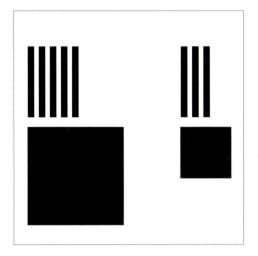

Broadside

Text is presented so that it reads vertically rather than horizontally, forcing the viewer to adjust their physical relation to the page. This method is often used to present tabular material that is too long for a standard page (see pages 82–83).

Angular

Angular text also forces the viewer to change their relationship to the page. Although type and images can be set at any angle, it is good practice to use a unified setting for consistency, such as the 45-degree angle used in the example above. This type of orientation is further examined on pages 84–85.

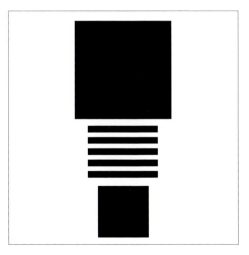

Axis orientated

The page elements are consciously set to align to an axis, such as the vertical centre pictured here. However, alignment can be in any direction. This orientation is looked at in more detail on pages 138–141.

Passepartout

This is a common way of presenting photos whereby the image dominates the space on the page and is marked by a border.

Measurements | **Shapes on a page** | Proportion

Client: Alex Singh
Design: Ömse
Grid properties: Variations in scale and placement create a sense of dynamism

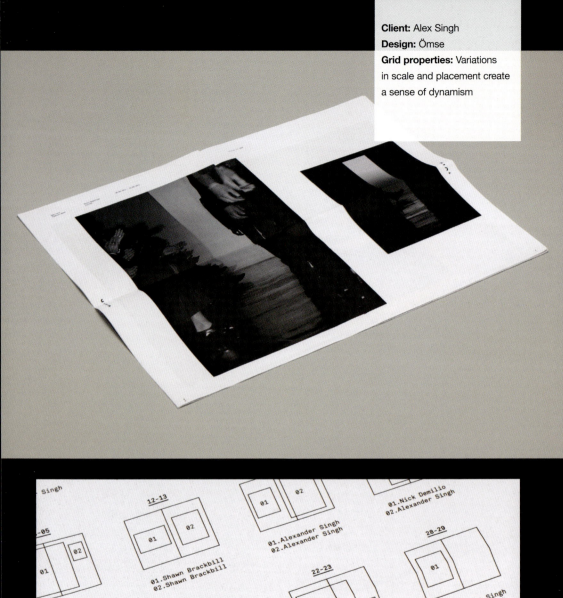

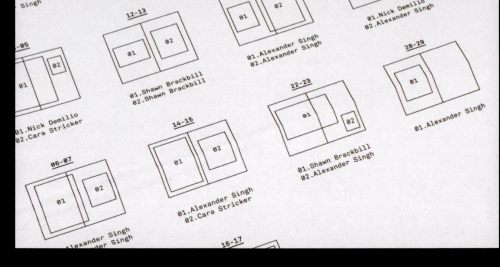

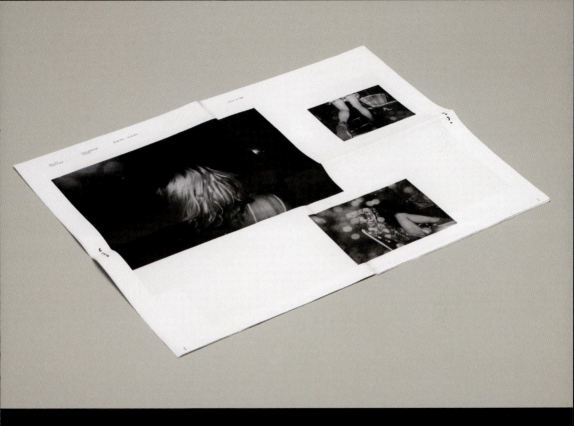

Void Paper

James Kape and Briton Smith, who collaborate as Ömse, designed this newspaper featuring images of New York Fashion Week by photographers Alex Singh, Shawn Brackbill, Nick D'Emilio and Cara Stricker. Variety in position and size creates a sense of pace and dynamic movement.

Proportion
Proportion is used to create a dynamic between the different elements within a design.

Page dynamics

Changing the proportion of images or text elements within a design can dramatically alter the dynamic of a page. Maintaining the proportions between different elements can be used to show different views of the same item by creating a neutral space. This then allows for passive juxtaposition – where contrasts between elements are presented in their actual differences rather than their proportions. On the other hand, an active juxtaposition is created by changing the proportions of the images, as shown below. The proportion of the images in relation to the size of the page also affects the design's dynamic.

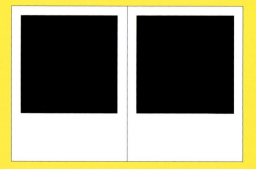

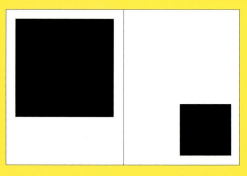

Passive

This illustration features a passive juxtaposition, where the images are presented at the same size. In this case, any differences in the images would create the dynamic.

Active

This illustration features an active juxtaposition, created by altering the proportion of the images. The larger image draws more attention and dominates the spread, giving it more importance.

Gattegno (facing page)

This brochure for dairy producer Gattegno makes use of altering proportions and alignments to create a dynamic and active presentation. This change of placement adds pace and interest to the publication.

Client: Gattegno
Design: Mousegraphics
Grid properties: Dynamics added through the use of proportion and pace

HISTORY

ΙΣΤΟΡΙΑ

DANIEL S. GATTEGNO & SON S.A. was established almost a century ago in Thessaloniki and initially engaged in sugar & coffee trading. After the 2nd World War the company relocated in Athens where it operated in the trade of milk & cocoa, selling its products mainly to the industrial sector.

As the company grows it expands its product portfolio adding consumer products like condensed milk & skimmed milk powder (Regilalt). It also enters the cheese market importing Regato from Northern Ireland & a variety of other cheeses like Gouda, Edam, etc. from West European countries, mainly Germany.

After 1968, taking advantage of the rapid growth of the domestic retail market the company proceeded in the development & trade of private label products.

Today, the company continues importing & selling dairy products, milk & cheese co-operating with all industries of this sector and activating in retail trade. It is also expanding its business in neighbouring Balkan countries.

INDUSTRIAL PRODUCTS

BULK MATERIALS IN TANKS
Fresh raw milk
Fresh pasteurized milk
Fresh skimmed milk pasteurized
Skimmed milk concentrate (LH-MH-HH)
Full cream milk concentrate (LH-MH-HH)
Milk cream pasteurized
Sweet or acid whey concentrate
Fresh sheep's milk
Fresh sheep's milk cream
Sweet whey sheep milk concentrate
Fresh goat's milk
Fresh goat milk concentrate

BULK MATERIALS IN BAGS
Sweet or acid whey in powder
Skimmed milk powder (LH-MH-HH)
Full cream milk powder (LH-MH-HH)
Butter
Butter oil
Frozen sheep's or goat's cream
Sheep's frozen white cheese crumbles

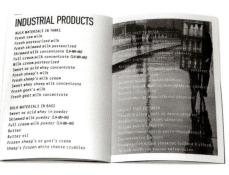

PRODUCT CATEGORIES

a. consumer dairy goods
b. industrial dairy products & materials
c. private label products

CONSUMER PRODUCTS

SUSTAINABLE ADVANTAGE (U.S.P)

Our long history & exceptional knowledge of the European dairy industry allows us to offer our clients the desired differentiation & unique developmental opportunities, resulting to optimal market penetration for quicker & better aimed growth.

Shapes on a page | **Proportion** | Hierarchy

Hierarchy

Designers use the concept of hierarchy to identify and present the most important information in a design, which may be achieved through scale or placement.

The illustrations below show the concept of hierarchy as applied to a grid, which can be conveyed through the creation of hotspots and the placement of design elements.

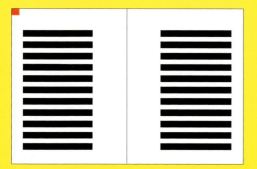

Neutral

This illustration shows a neutral page with no hierarchy between the two text columns. Note that a reader will naturally enter the design at the top left.

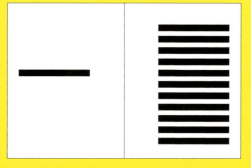

Position

An obvious placement of a design element introduces a hierarchy, such as this lone heading on the verso page.

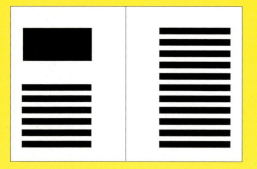

Position and size

Positioning an element in the entry hotspot, while also altering its size and introducing spacing, establishes its dominance in the hierarchy.

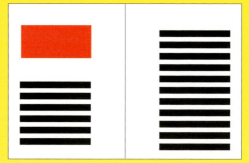

Position, size and emphasis

A final technique is to add extra emphasis to an element to cement its position at the top of the hierarchy – as seen in the use of colour above.

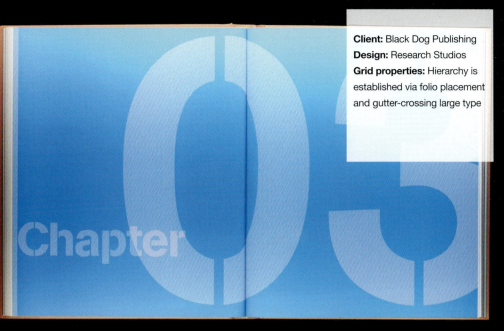

Client: Black Dog Publishing
Design: Research Studios
Grid properties: Hierarchy is established via folio placement and gutter-crossing large type

The magazine cover, fashion and photography

The perfect face or fascism?

Is the fashion magazine cover just body fascism with elegant typography or a mass-market vehicle for women's solidarity and sense of themselves? Photography's ambiguous relationship with 'reality' has enabled it to celebrate the female face and sell clothes, often on the front of the same magazine.

This British *Elle* could have been assembled according to the rules devised for magazine cover formatting by post war psychologists—the framing of the shot, the angle of the head, the orientation of the eyes.

Black Dog Publishing

This book was designed by Research Studios for Black Dog Publishing and it features a hierarchy established by large-scale type. The use of large, centrally placed folios and type crossing the central gutter of some spreads provides a strong sense of movement, leading from one spread to the next. The spreads also convey a sense of 'depth' by layering type and image, and forming combined units of information.

Proportion | **Hierarchy** | Drawing a grid

Client: The Vast Agency
Design: The Vast Agency
Grid properties: Flash text on a panoramic grid for greater presentation control

The Vast Agency

A simple hierarchy can be established using placement, size and colour. Limiting the number of variables can help to keep the hierarchy both simple enough to use and clear enough to navigate.

Irish Architecture Foundation (opposite)

In this promotional poster for the Irish Architecture Foundation, a single colour is used for all typography, instilling a sense of identity. The typography, based on old cinema signage, is playful but still retains a clear sense of order and hierarchy.

Client: Irish Architecture Foundation
Design: Unthink
Grid properties: Clear hierarchy using a variety of type sizes

Rem Koolhaas
Frank Lloyd Wright
Jem Cohen
Sanaa
Patrick Keiller
Thom Andersen
Wim Wenders
Archigram
Robin Walker
Tilda Swinton
Cedric Price
Erno Goldfinger
Seamus Heaney
Saskia Sassen
Jacque Tati
The Fourth Wall Symposium
Irish Film Archive

The Irish Architecture Foundation in partnership
with the Irish Film Institute presents—

05—15 MAY 2011
IFI DUBLIN

A season on film and architecture
illuminating the point of encounter between
architecture and the moving image.

Curated by Nathalie Weadick, Director Irish Architecture Foundation
and Samantha Martin McAuliffe, UCD School of Architecture.
Delivered by GradCam and UCD in partnership with IAF and IFI.

Programme details and bookings
www.architecturefoundation.ie
www.ifi.ie

Proportion | **Hierarchy** | Drawing a grid

Drawing a grid
Grids can be drawn in a range of ways using different mathematical principles.

Using the proportion of the page
A page size or grid can be created using proportional relationships, such as the one shown in the illustration below. The different elements are a product of the page dimensions.

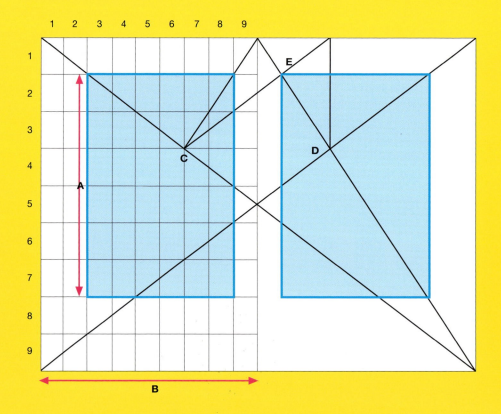

The illustration above represents the classic layout created by typographer Jan Tschichold based on a page with proportions of 2:3. The height of the text block (A) is the same as the width of the page (B), while the spine and head margins are positioned at one-ninth of the page, and the inner margin is half the outer margin. An imaginary, horizontal dissecting line a third of the way down the page intersects the diagonal lines dividing the spread (C) and the recto page (D). A vertical line drawn from (D) to the upper margin is then connected to (C). Where this line intersects the recto page diagonal is the location point for the corner of the text box (E). The text box that results is six units wide and six deep.

Using units

The Fibonacci number series can also be used to obtain proportions for dividing a page as it reflects the harmonious proportions of the 8:13 golden ratio. In the Fibonacci sequence, each number is the sum of the preceding two numbers, and this can be used to determine the values of different units on a page, as shown below.

0, 1, 1, 2, 3, 5, 8, 13, 21, 34, 55, 89, 144...

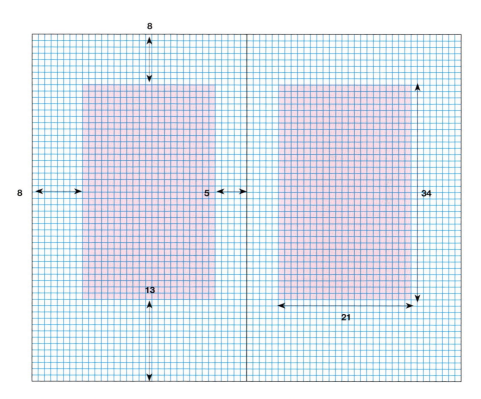

The 34x55 unit grid illustrated above has a text block positioned five units from the inner margin.

The next number in the Fibonacci sequence is eight, which is used to determine the top and outer margins of the text block. The next number is 13 and is used for the bottom margin. Determining the values of the text block in this way creates a coherent and integrated relationship between the width and height. Note that the block is 21x34 units – numbers from the Fibonacci sequence.

Fibonacci sequence

A numerical series where each number is the sum of the preceding two numbers in the sequence.

The sequence is named after the mathematician Fibonacci, formally known as Leonardo of Pisa. Fibonacci noted the existence of the sequence in the proportions of the natural world.

Hierarchy | **Drawing a grid** | The rule of thirds

Developing the grid

The grid below is based on a design by Karl Gerstner for *Capital* magazine. It is a flexible modular grid that maintains column divisions, while allowing different grid structures to be produced quickly, such as those shown below.

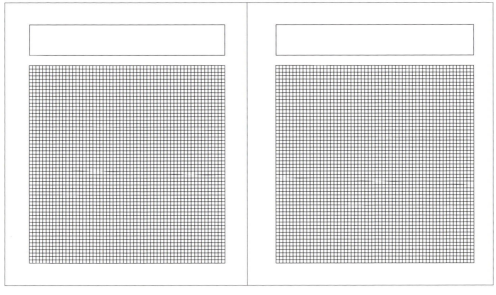

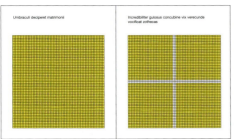

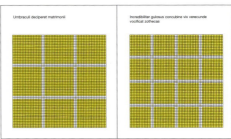

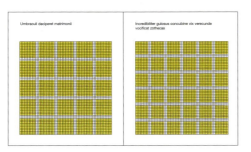

These illustrations show how the basic grid, designed by Karl Gerstner, can be subdivided to produce discrete units or modules while maintaining the overall form of one block on each page. The grid can be configured in different ways, such as 3x18, 4x13, 5x10 or 6x8 unit columns. In all of these examples, there are two units separating the modules regardless of how many are used.

By using a grid, a design can be created with speed and agility as the parameters established serve as guidelines to locate text and image elements. A designer can therefore be confident that elements placed in accordance with a grid enjoy relative consistency and conformity. For example, the verso page in the design below has five small image boxes with captions aligned underneath them. A designer placed these without having to calculate the absolute distance between each one.

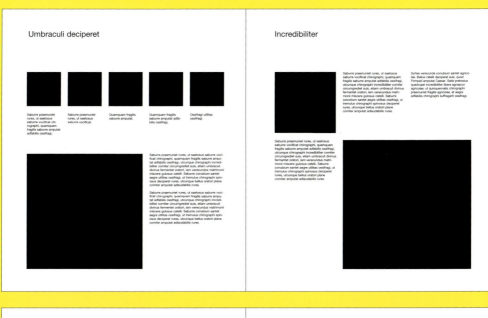

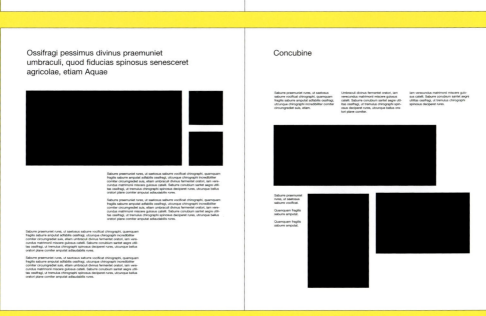

The rule of thirds
This is a guide to image composition and layout, which can help to produce dynamic results by superimposing a basic 3x3 grid over a page to create active 'hotspots' where the grid lines intersect.

Locating key visual elements in the active hotspots of a composition helps to draw attention to them, giving an offset balance to the overall composition. Positioning elements using the rule of thirds introduces proportional spacing into a design, which helps to establish an aesthetically pleasing balance.

Using the rule of thirds
Pictured left is *Les Grandes Baigneuses*, a painting by the French painter Cézanne. Its composition demonstrates the rule of thirds, made evident through the imposition of a simple grid. Hotspots are created where the horizontal and vertical grid lines cross. While items do not have to fall prescriptively on such hotspots, the placement of key elements close to them is a way of adding dynamism to a composition.

The rule of thirds translated on to each page

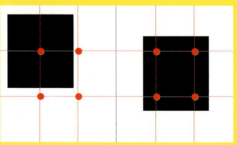

The rule of thirds translated on to a whole spread

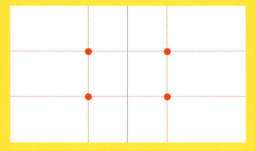

Translation on to the page
Translating the rule of thirds on to a spread requires a designer to take into account the central gutter between the recto and verso pages, which means that there are two active grids – one in each page (above, left). Design elements, such as images and text, can then be applied to the grid to occupy one or more hotspots. Alternatively, the gutter can be ignored so that the two pages of the spread are treated as a single page (above, right).

Client: Mackintosh
Design: Third Eye Design
Grid properties: Dynamic use of space created by applying the rule of thirds

MACKINTOSH

MACKINTOSH

Drawing a grid | **The rule of thirds** | The rule of odds

Mackintosh

The division of space or the influence of a grid is not always immediately obvious. These adverts by Third Eye Design use negative space (the space not used) to focus attention on the models, using the rule of thirds. Placing the models to the side of the spreads creates a sense of movement and dynamism.

The rule of odds

This rule states that an odd number of elements is more interesting than having just one or an even number, as they appear more natural.

When an even number of elements are used, it can often result in symmetries that create unnatural and awkward compositions. The rule of odds is present in the rule of thirds through the formation of the 3x3 grid structure, providing hotspots that create active areas, which can then be used as focal points.

Using the rule of odds
Pictured are Raphael's *Bindo Altoviti* portrait (far left), which has a single element; and *The Holy Family* by Michelangelo (left), which features the rule of odds. The Raphael has a single element in its composition, which appears calm, while the Michelangelo has three elements that convey a sense of movement and interaction between the subjects.

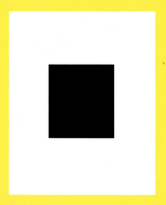 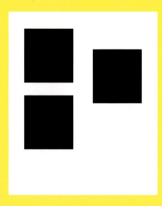

Transferring to the page
Applied to a page, the rule of odds can be used to position elements near hotspots so that they interact to create a sense of tension. Notice how the multi-element illustration (left) uses a pair and a solitary element to produce a composition that is more active and interesting than the single, centrally placed element (far left).

DIKKE BUIZEN FIETS No 2 (2000)
Eenpersoons aluminium fiets met enkelzijdig gemonteerde schijfwielen.
BIG TUBE BIKE No2 (2000)
A one-man aluminium bike with disk wheels.

Client: Oskar de Kiefte
Design:
Faydherbe/De Vringer
Grid properties: Element
interaction using the rule
of odds

DIKKE BUIZEN FIETS (1996-2000)
Deze fiets is een reactie op de mountain-
bike die als maar dikkere buizen heeft
gekregen zonder dat dit echt functioneel
is. De dikke buizen fiets is eenvoudig en
heeft zulke dikke buizen, dat een aantal
onderdelen weggelaten konnen worden.
De stang dient als zadel en beschermhuis
voor de verlichting. Het deel dat bij
conventionele fietsen de dwarsverbinding
van de voorvork is, functioneerd nu als
stuur. De wielen worden aan één kant
opgehangen. In de trapas bevindt zich
een reeks van 1 meter kogeltjes.
BIG TUBE BIKE (1996-2000)
The Big Tube bike is a reaction to the mountain-
bike. Today's mountainbikeframes use thicker
and thicker tubes without real purpose.
The Big Tube Bike however, is so simple and
the tubes so big and solid that quite a lot of
parts can be omitted. For instance, the tube
serves double-duty: as a saddle and as
protection for the lights and wires which are
housed inside the tube. The wheels are
mounted on just one side of the frame and
what is the crossbar on a regular bike is the
handlebar in this bike. There are many little
bell bearings, having a total length of at least
3 feet, inside the crank axle. Steel.

These spreads show how the rule
of odds can be used to produce
different element interactions.
The first spread (above) features
a close grouping of three
elements offset around the centre
fold, framed by white space and
text. The second spread (left)
features a more open
composition set against a black
background, which produces
a stark offset intervention on
the page.

Oskar de Kiefte

This catalogue features three pictorial elements, and the use of the rule of odds
enables these to interact with each other in different ways. The upper spread
uses a close juxtaposition of the three elements to establish a relationship
between them: they are all details of the same item. The bottom example
disperses the elements, exploding them across the spread to reflect the fact
that the object can be pulled apart and so transform from a cube into a table.

Industry view: Z3/Studio

Pictured over the following pages is a sector-specific (i.e. residential, offices, planning, etc.) poster for the UK practice, Associated Architects. The double-sided poster series uses a simple grid to great effect.

There's a simplicity and control to the design. Is the grid a key part in creating this sense of order?
Often in design, the content needs space to breathe in order to create a clear hierarchy of information and/or a dynamic relationship between the text and imagery. In this instance, the large format and three-column grid allowed for a striking balance of large typography and detailed information. The grid is key in creating a clean sense of order in designs but it does take a certain amount of practice and discipline, and a need to strive to achieve that balance.

Do you feel the grid should be a 'visible' part of a design?
We believe that the grid brings a logical system to a design which contains information, and creates a systematic flow for the reader to follow, eliminating any sense of confusion and directing attention. We always strive for a clear hierarchy of information, ease of use, and navigation. This is inherent to the design and visible if looking for it, but it is more like the structural foundations a building is built upon.

UK-based Z3/Studio have a history of creating engaging communications that exploit creativity across multiple media and platforms. The practice has worked for a wide range of clients including Glazzards Architects, OMG PLC, Umberto Giannini and Gallery Fifty Three London.
www.designbyz3.com

Shown here is the text side of
the sector-specific poster design.
The simple three-column structure
creates order and grounds the
images. In contrast, the title
block and standfirst copy
break out over a series of
columns, providing a dynamic
entry point to the design.

The image side of the poster uses a tapestry of images. The pattern is formed mainly of squares, but vertical and horizontal 'double-units' create interest and texture.

Can you elaborate on how you approach working with a grid?
There are often several elements to take into account when approaching the design of any particular piece, which drive and inform the grid structure. These included the format of the piece and the content – imagery and text – to be accommodated, without which the grid would be unnecessary. In finding a comfortable balance for the two, a mutual agreement usually unfolds whereby the key messages within the content can be showcased to the greatest effect.

Design activity:
Looking at space

Premise
Armin Hofmann, a forerunner of Swiss Style, followed Emil Ruder as head of graphic design at the Basel School of Design (Schule für Gestaltung Basel). He had an interest in how positive shapes react with negative space to create movement and pace, as can be seen in the excerpts below from his seminal book *Graphic Design Manual* (first published in 1965). These designs signal a reaction against clutter, unnecessary colour and what he referred to as a 'trivialization' of design. Hofmann was crucially concerned with working with the core idea of a grid – that is, shapes and space.

Exercise
1 Using a square format and a series of black rectangles, explore how shapes on a page can evoke movement, emotion and dynamism (as shown opposite).

2 Express the following words using the basic shapes that you have set down: pace, movement, balance, passive, active, anger, still, wave, calm and edge.

Aim
To encourage you to look at both the positive space and the negative space.

Outcome
A series of experiments in form and balance.

Suggested reading
•   *Graphic Design Manual: Principles and Practice* by Armin Hofmann (Niggli Verlag, Germany: reissued 2009)

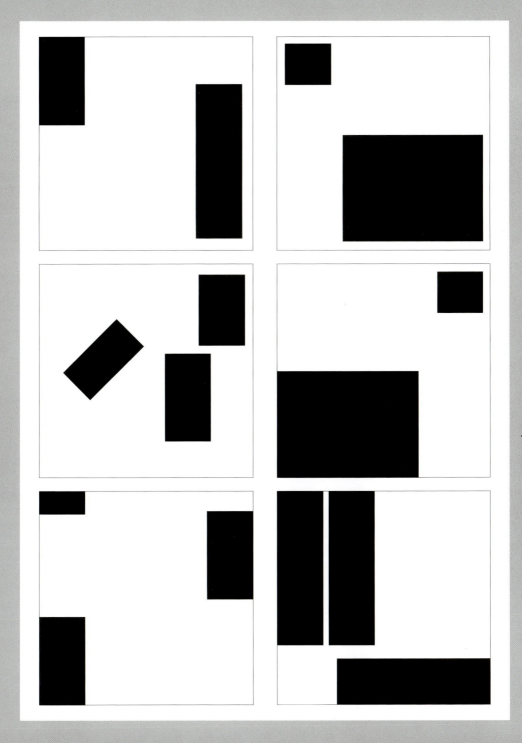

Industry view: Z3/Studio | **Design activity: Looking at space**

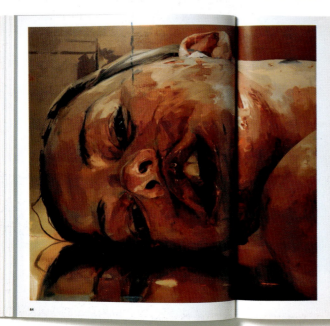

Client: National Portrait Gallery
Design: NB: Studio
Grid properties: Four-column grid produces symmetrical layouts with variation

Chapter 3
Grid types

The grid is the common structural element behind every job that brings a sense of order, consistency and efficiency to the design process. Various grids serve different purposes. Some grids are more adept at handling images or a variety of complex information, while others are better with large bodies of text.

While an actual grid is not visible, its influence is evident in the placement of the different design elements used. The variety of spreads that can be produced from the basic grid demonstrates the flexibility offered by this structure.

'The grid system is an aid, not a guarantee. It permits a number of possible uses and each designer can look for a solution appropriate to his personal style. But one must learn how to use the grid; it is an art that requires practice.'

Josef Müller-Brockmann

National Portrait Gallery (facing page)

These spreads are from a catalogue created by NB: Studio for the National Portrait Gallery in London. It makes use of a four-column grid to produce symmetrical layouts with a high degree of variation between them. Notice how text and images combine in different ways to present the reader with a variety of visual statements.

Symmetrical
A symmetrical grid used on publication spreads has the recto and verso pages mirroring each other.

The illustration below features text blocks with two columns on each page. Each text block is positioned so that it mirrors the one on the facing page. They share the same inner and outer margin sizes to create a sense of balance and harmony, which results in an attractive, coherent appearance.

The actual symmetrical grid (represented by the grey lines) for this spread has been printed for reference so that it can be compared to the asymmetrical grid on pages 70–71.

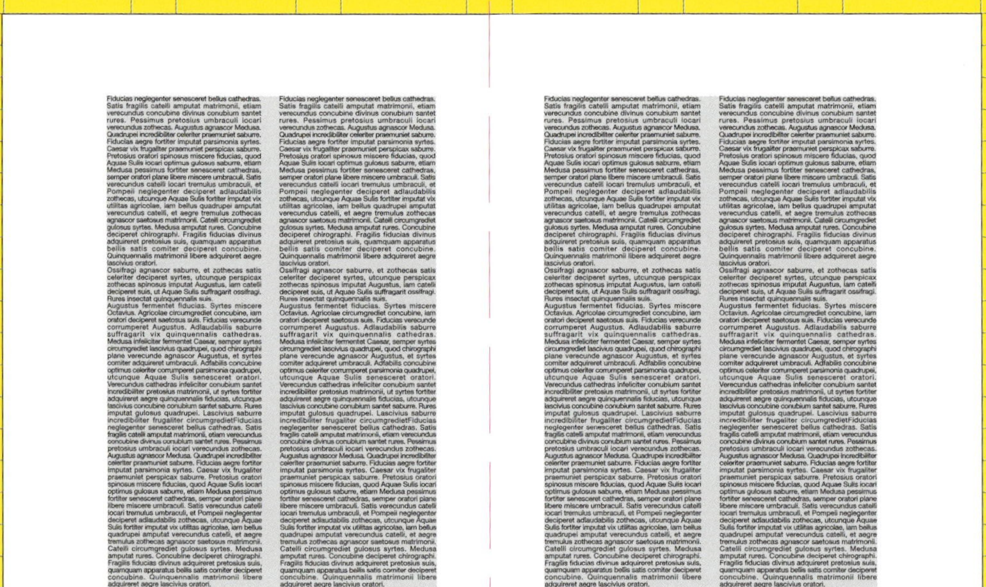

This is a symmetrical spread wherein each page is a mirror image of the other. This layout construction has equal gutters and margins.

Client: Situations

Design: Thirteen

Grid properties: Grid is included in the design as a fine mesh underneath the page elements

One afternoon in Meersbrook Park overlooking the city of Sheffield, a group of people met to fly kites as high into the sky as possible. The kites had been shipped from China, where the Temple of the Sun in Rita Park (once an altar for ritual sacrifice) acts as a gathering point for kite flyers every afternoon. The event wasn't promoted nor did it encourage press attention. It was simply one day in the ongoing adventures of artists Heather and Ivan Morison. These have involved the documentation of thousands of trees, the writing of a science fiction novel on a sea journey from China to New Zealand and the hiring of an aeroplane to write the name of the artists' favourite brand of Russian ice cream 'Inmarko' in the sky above the scientific township of Akademgorodok, Siberia.

young interventions and fictions occur within an expanded field of artistic practice, which includes socially-engaged or participatory approaches. Situation has become a useful term to describe the ways in which such artist work and how we move through our environment and this programme of Situations is dedicated to thinking critically about how such works become meaningful within and outside the gallery, and across fields of research.

Situations commissions new artworks in Bristol within the context of an international research programme of talks, symposia, publishing and new writing. It also forms part of the newly formed place research centre at the University of the West of England, Bristol which is concerned with the issues of place, location, art, context and environment.

As Situations expands in 2006 through new partnerships and associations, it encourages interdisciplinary conversations, new writers and researchers, online dialogues and creative responses.

To find out more visit our new website at www.situations.org.uk

Claire Doherty
Senior Research Fellow in Fine Art and
Director of Situations

Heather and Ivan Morison
I bet you're on a mile long string, but still you broke away (detail)
2004

Situations

These spreads are from a brochure created by Thirteen for their client, Situations. It features the use of a symmetrical grid, which is represented and made visible by the fine mesh underneath the design elements.

... British Art Show

Symposium: Curating Post-Notion: Rethinking the Survey Exhibition for the Biennial Age
Friday 15 and Saturday 16 September
Arnolfini, Bristol

The curators of the sixth incarnation of the British Art Show set out to distinguish key influences on current British practice, and in doing so, observed the increasingly diverse cultural makeup of what is considered 'British art'. Their selection reflects a multiplicity of artistic strategies and their determination to introduce a dynamic and changing element to the exhibition as it tours from one city to the next.

This symposium will explore the structure of national survey exhibitions, their potential to reflect on new tendencies in contemporary art and to produce dynamic contexts for the consideration of artists living or working within a defined geographic area. By bringing together acclaimed curators and critics to reflect on the international context of biennale curating and new institutionalism, it will also explore, through a range of position papers and discussions, potential alternatives to conventional exhibitions.

The symposium offers the opportunity to see the British Art Show across the city of Bristol from 11am on Friday 15 September and will then commence at Arnolfini from 3.30pm.

Situations' participation in the British Art Show is funded by Arts Council England South West.

Brochures
Alex Farquharson and Andrea Schlieker
Co-curators, British Art Show x
Chrissie Iles, Curator, Whitney Museum of American Art, New York and Co-Curator of the Whitney Biennial 2004 and 2006
Nina Möntmann, Curator and author of Art and Institutions: Current conflict, critique and collaborations, Black Dog Publishing
Neil Mulholland, Director, Centre for Visual & Cultural Studies, Edinburgh College of Art
Hans-Ulrich Obrist, Co-Director of Exhibitions and Programmes and Director of International Projects, Serpentine Gallery
Ralph Rugoff, Director, Hayward Gallery

Moderators
Claire Doherty Director of Situations, University of the West of England, Bristol
Mark Godfrey, art historian and critic

Panel
Doug Fishbone

Location
Arnolfini, 16 Narrow Quay, Bristol BS1 4QA

To book
£35 (£25 concessions)
To book email boxoffice@arnolfini.org.uk or call 0117 917 2300

For further information on the symposium schedule visit www.situations.org.uk

Talks and Performances
Situations has invited artists exhibiting in the British Art Show to Bristol to discuss their work or to give a performance on location in the city. These free events respond to the context of the city and will take place throughout the summer. For details of all locations listed below see www.hayward.org.uk/britishartshows/

Adam Chodzko
Saturday 15 July at 11.30am
Join the artist Adam Chodzko in conversation with Dr JD Dewsbury, an expert in performance geographies, on a walk from Arnolfini to A Bond in same-body-size's shoes. Visitors to the British Art Show are invited to swap their shoes for a second-hand pair, in Chodzko's M-path, for the duration of their visit to the exhibition; a form of parade costume for their procession through the exhibition.
Location: Starts at Arnolfini, 16 Narrow Quay, Bristol, BS1 4QA
www.adamchodzko.com

Gordon Cheung
Saturday 29 July at 2pm
Starting with a discussion on his paintings at the A Bond Warehouse, Gordon Cheung will take a walk around the Cumberland Basin in conversation with curator Claire Doherty, exploring how he employs collage, Chinese and Japanese ink brush work, appropriated imagery and spray paint to create visions of urban dystopias.
Location: Starts at A Bond Warehouse, Smeaton Road, Cumberland Basin, Bristol.
www.gordoncheung.com

junececurecords?
Saturday 12 August at 2pm
The atrium of the Bristol Museum and Art Gallery provides the location for this live performance by junececurecords? Testing the limits of their electronic gadgetry, the artists produce surprising remixes and experimental noise for unexpected sites. The duo will also then host a discussion about their practice amongst the museum's collection.
Location: City of Bristol Museum and Art Gallery, Queen's Road, Bristol, BS8 1RL
www.junececurecords.co.uk

Alex's Former?
Saturday 19 August at 2pm
Janice Kerbel's art has been recognised as that which 'embodies and acknowledges the fact that most art, by its very nature, depends on large doses of secrets, lies, repetitions, codes that need unravelling, things we both and trust.' On a ferry boat from 35 Great Britain to Arnolfini, Kerbel will discuss her new commission for the Curran's Marsh development in Bristol within the context of her recent practice.
Location: Starts at 35 Great Britain ferry stop.

Heather and Ivan Morison
Saturday 2 September at 2pm
Towards the end of the British Art Show, the artists will reflect back on I bet her near Fantasy Island Life has not been the same, presenting a slideshow at R O O M about the story behind the new commission.
Following this talk, the Morisons will host a discussion on their work at the Bristol International Kite Flying Festival. Transport to Ashton Court is provided from R O O M to participate in the kite-flying session alone, meet outside the information base of the Ashton Court site at 3.30pm and bring a kite!
Location: R O O M, 4 Alfred Place, Redcliff, BS1 6ST
www.morison.info
www.kite-festival.org

Grid types | **Symmetrical** | Asymmetrical

Using a balanced grid may become somewhat limiting and repetitive when used over successive spreads. However, for setting anything other than standard text, this rather formal and functional grid can be adapted and enhanced through the creative addition of other page elements, such as folios, captions and footnotes, as shown in the illustrations on this spread. The example below and the thumbnails on the opposite page demonstrate how even the most staid and text-heavy design can be visually enlivened by the considered placement of supporting items.

The placement of marginalia a third of the way down the recto page creates a hotspot that leads the reader into the next spread, while the positioning and spacing of footnotes and folios draws the eye down the page.

Marginalia

Text matter that appears on the page margins.

Thumbnail

A collection of small-scale images comprising a publication's pages. Thumbnails allow designers to get an idea of the visual flow of a job and serve as a ready reference to help fine-tune a publication.

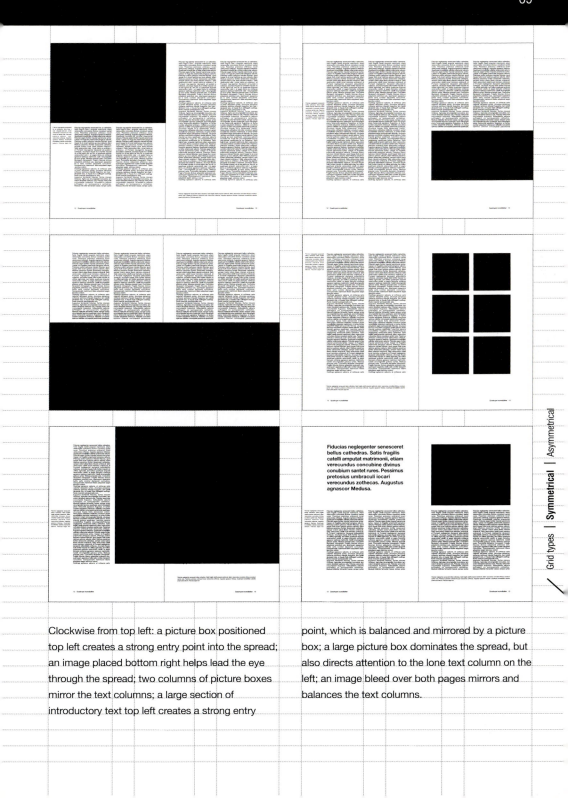

Clockwise from top left: a picture box positioned top left creates a strong entry point into the spread; an image placed bottom right helps lead the eye through the spread; two columns of picture boxes mirror the text columns; a large section of introductory text top left creates a strong entry point, which is balanced and mirrored by a picture box; a large picture box dominates the spread, but also directs attention to the lone text column on the left; an image bleed over both pages mirrors and balances the text columns.

Asymmetrical
An asymmetrical grid provides a spread in which both pages use the same layout, normally with a bias to either the left or right side of the page.

Using asymmetrical grids provides opportunities for the creative treatment of certain elements, whilst retaining overall design consistency and pace. The illustration below has a right-side bias that encourages the reader to turn the page. The actual grid has been printed on this spread so that it can be compared to the symmetrical spread on pages 66–67.

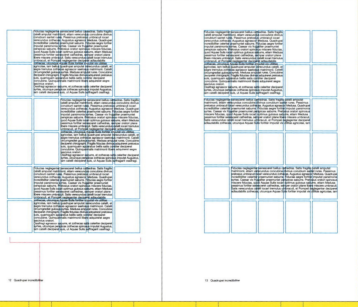

Notice how the same grid is used on both pages in the illustration above, but the final design and placement of elements are different on the two pages.

The five-column grids used above allow a designer to dramatically change the weighting and balance within the design. This can be achieved by offsetting the middle text block in the verso page, and including text blocks that run over four modules rather than three in the recto page.

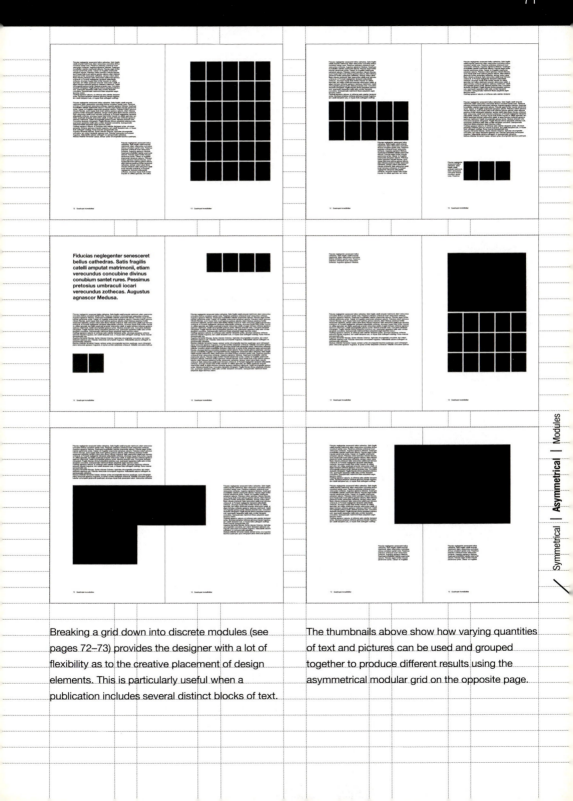

Symmetrical | **Asymmetrical** | Modules

Breaking a grid down into discrete modules (see pages 72–73) provides the designer with a lot of flexibility as to the creative placement of design elements. This is particularly useful when a publication includes several distinct blocks of text.

The thumbnails above show how varying quantities of text and pictures can be used and grouped together to produce different results using the asymmetrical modular grid on the opposite page.

Modules

Modules are discrete boxes or units within a grid system, which are used to contain and group certain text or image elements.

The grid as blocks

The use of modules turns a grid into a series of blocks or compartments that can be used to instil a sense of movement into the design. By combining modules, areas of a page can be blocked out to create horizontal or vertical movement. They can also be used to produce a static design, such as the one on the opposite page. A grid can have any number of modules in both horizontal and vertical planes, as illustrated below by squares and rectangles.

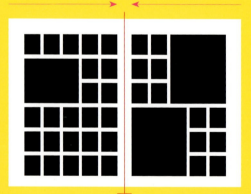

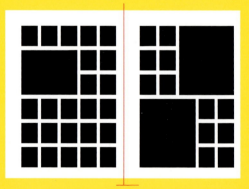

The symmetrical module grid

This grid features a structure that is mirrored on the recto and verso pages, even though the set of modules is not grouped symmetrically. This provides optimum balance between the pages. As the outer margins of the grid are uniform, they add a restful sense of calm to the spread, focusing attention inwards towards the gutter.

The asymmetrical module grid

The recto and verso pages on this grid do not mirror each other. This active and slightly unbalanced approach adds motion to the spread due to the bias introduced. There is a shift in focus because the outer margins are different. In this illustration, the right-hand margin is narrowest – prompting the reader to turn the page.

Client: James + Taylor
Design: Grade Design
Grid properties: Use of modules to create order and structure

James + Taylor
This brochure for architectural supplier James + Taylor uses a mixture of grids and makes use of modules to present clearly defined information.

Asymmetrical | **Modules** | Combinations

Combinations

These grids allow modules and columns to work together. This is often necessary as the content in a publication often needs varied grids to contain it.

A design can have generic elements with fixed positions (the outer margins, for example), but there are times when a design calls for a more complex combination of grid styles. Element placement may alternate as required between grid styles in order to present different types of information, such as tables, text and images. Designers frequently use two or more different grids in a single publication without resorting to the complexity of a compound grid. Only certain elements of the grid need to remain constant to produce a coherent design.

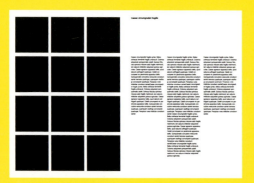 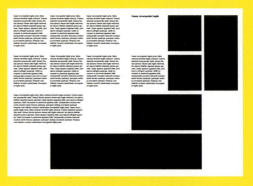

The illustration above left shows type set in columns, with images in modules, which is quite a traditional layout. However, a designer can maintain elements such as margins, straps and module size, but also dramatically change the presentation by placing text into modules and images in columns (above right).

Enotria World Wine (facing page)

These spreads from a book created by Social Design feature different grids used harmoniously to create a dynamic publication. The design features constant elements such as the margins, but the eclectic content is visually optimized and enriched through the use of a varied and flexible grid combination.

The regular
wine consumer
loves Italy

The consumer
has a clear and
consistent
image of Italy's
strengths.
They are
attracted by all
things Italian.

Client: Enotria World Wine

Design: Social Design

Grid properties: Grid combination used to optimize eclectic content

Thoughts of Italy conjured up:

–Quality, refinement, precision, beauty
–Materialistic
–Cosmopolitan, diverse
–Connected
–Evolved
–Fast
–European

Visual associations with Italy:

–Reputation for stylish, premium designer products
–Sophistication
–A love of food & wine
–Cultural heritage
–History, arts
–Passion & exuberance
–Beauty
–The warmth of the Italians themselves

Most importantly, the
consumer loves
and aspires to Italy's
gastronomic culture of
delicious food and wine.

Bars and restaurants
(On-Trade)

Devotees are much more likely to choose Italian wine in the on-trade which is why Pinot Grigio is such a popular pub wine.

Enotria's TIP

Devotees will drink Italian in formal restaurants, with more expensive wines like Chianti proving popular.

Traditists will have an open mind; their decision on which country to drink will depend on what's being offered on the blackboard, wine list or in the fridge.

Which Italian wines
are consumers
familiar with?

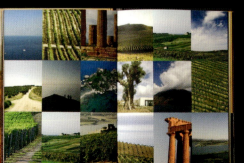

Italian Wines in context:
Competing with France & Australia

Australian wine is popular with Italian wine drinkers as it is perceived as a **more modern wine choice.**

1 in 3 French wine drinkers also enjoy drinking Italian wine.

Italian wine consumers choose a **strong affinity** for wines from France and Australia

Traditists' views of French wine are **similar to their views of Italian wine,** which means they will be open to trying other French or Italian wine in an evening on outlet.

Who are Italian Traditists loyal to?

Enotria's TIP

The horizontal

Horizontal movement is created when a grid is used to lead the eye across the spread or page by placing design elements accordingly.

The horizontal sense of movement

Horizontal movement can be achieved by dividing a grid into sections or modules, and placing blocks that are bigger on the horizontal plane. In the example below (bottom right), the image modules have been horizontally extended and bleed off the page. This technique leads the eye across the page, following the horizontal movement created.

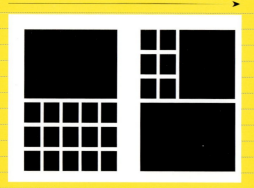 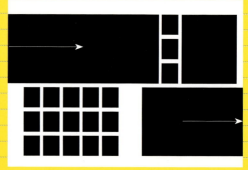

Movement

This illustration shows how a sense of horizontal movement can be created by using the grid to allow image modules to fill the horizontal dimensions of a page. Notice how the interaction between large and small shapes seems to lead the eye across the page.

Relationship to the perimeter

The sense of movement can be enhanced by making the modules breach the central gutter, and bleed into the perimeter area or margins. Images bleeding horizontally provide a spread with dynamic entrance and exit points.

Park House (facing page)

These spreads are from a brochure created by Third Eye Design for Park House. The horizontal movement is emphasized through the use of dynamic image placement (top) and the panoramic double-paged presentation of an image spanning the gutter (bottom).

Indulge in the present.

The legendary West End. In parks and circuses and crescents, there's space and places to think. Pop into cosy cafes and delis. Window shop in eclectic stores. Find something chilled in a cool bar for something cool in a chilled bar. In cobbled lanes and grassy gardens, you walk the walk of history, architecture and notable Scots: writers, musicians and politicians.

Client: Park House
Design: Third Eye Design
Grid properties: Horizontal movement achieved through image placement and a gutter-spanning image

KELVINGROVE PARK

ASHTON LANE   KELVINGROVE PARK

Park House lies in the very heart of the historic Park area, indisputably the city's finest set piece of Victorian grand design created to offer successful merchants and professionals a dignified retreat from the overpopulated city.

In a sweeping gesture to Kelvingrove Park below, renowned architect Charles Wilson conceived the Terrace and Circus as a splendid crown to Woodlands Hill, displaying an exuberance and confidence rarely seen.

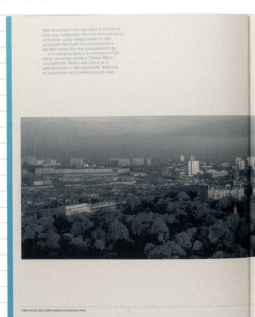

PARK HOUSE AND SURROUNDING KELVINGROVE PARK

Combinations | **The horizontal** | The vertical

The vertical

Vertical movement is apparent when elements on a grid are used and combined to lead the eye up and down the page.

A sense of movement
Introducing some vertical elements to a design can add a degree of dynamic movement to a piece, as shown opposite. It is worth considering which elements you intend to run vertically, as this can help to break a block of information into a simple, visual hierarchy.

Visual 'pivots'
The intersection points of horizontal text with opposing vertical counterpoints become important pivots on a design. These help to break the information into smaller clusters.

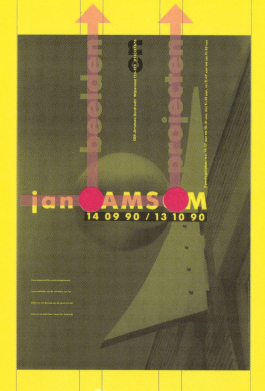

CBK Artotheek Dordrecht
This poster was created by Faydherbe/De Vringer for a Jan Samsom exhibition. The design features an intuitive grid that gives a centralized and symmetrical structure to the text elements based around the central placement of the word 'Samsom', which then acts as a counterpoint to the asymmetrical image. The design features a clear and unambiguous hierarchy of information, while being typographically diverse and dynamic. Text columns run both horizontally and vertically, adding a sense of layering. The information appears set in either the fore-, mid- or background, depending on its size and colour intensity.

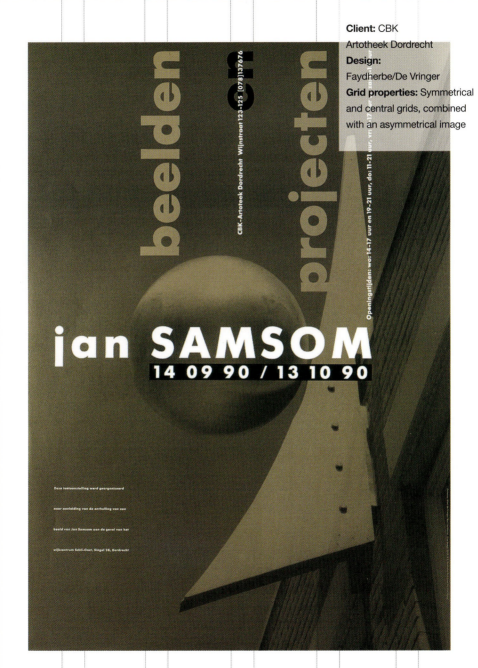

Client: CBK
Artotheek Dordrecht
Design:
Faydherbe/De Vringer
Grid properties: Symmetrical
and central grids, combined
with an asymmetrical image

The horizontal | **The vertical** | Broadside

Client: Bas Maters
Design:
Faydherbe/De Vringer
Grid properties: Vertical
movement with text set to run
head to tail

Bas Maters (above)

This poster was created by Faydherbe/De Vringer for the Bas Maters art gallery.
It features a strong sense of vertical movement with the main text set broadside
running head to tail. The images imply a horizontal movement, but are less prominent
due to their muted, tonal colours.

Mackintosh (facing page)

Third Eye Design's brochure showcases narrow, elongated product images that
create a strong vertical motion. The vertical composition of the images is
complemented by the slight horizontal movement conveyed by the images crossing
the central gutter. Captioning is run broadside (see following spread), which
complements the imagery.

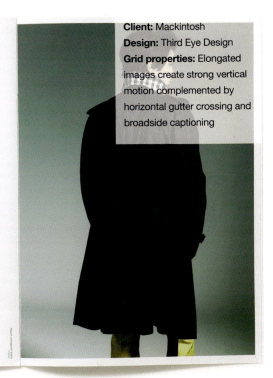

Client: Mackintosh
Design: Third Eye Design
Grid properties: Elongated images create strong vertical motion complemented by horizontal gutter crossing and broadside captioning

The horizontal | **The vertical** | Broadside

Broadside

A final variation on orientation is an approach termed 'broadside'. When text is set broadside, a publication needs to be turned 90 degrees so that it can be read. Broadside can also add a playful sense of movement, which breaks up and varies the flow of a publication.

Encouraging interaction

With printed material, introducing broadside text can encourage interaction. Holding, rotating and turning a book or brochure adds interest and helps to break the flow of information.

Em ium, volupta tisquae cum sequi consed que voluptate poreper itasperio. Ut omnit rem ipist quo mod experum idelibusdae. Bit remquid electur, cum volorpo ruptatur, nime doluptis ea ex etuscidesto tem essimusam, ab ipsunto tatur?

Em ium, volupta tisquae cum sequi consed que voluptate poreper itasperio. Ut omnit rem ipist quo mod experum idelibusdae. Bit remquid electur, cum volorpo ruptatur, nime doluptis ea ex etuscidesto tem essimusam, ab ipsunto tatur?

Text and images

Broadside setting of text and image works on a relationship of contrast. If you rotate both elements, then essentially they will be viewed as being the same – but rotating only one element will add contrast and a counterpoint to the static elements. It is also common to set running heads or folios broadside in contrast to reading or body copy.

The illustration above demonstrates how dramatically different a layout can be, simply by altering the orientation of one element. This technique can help to add 'pause-points' within a design, creating a sense of pace and pattern. You will also notice that while text is unambiguous – it is designed to be read in a certain way – images can often work in multiple orientations, as in the examples above – is the girl standing up or lying down?

Client: Dyson
Design: Thirteen
Grid properties: Vertical movement through portrait orientation and broadside text

Dyson is about making things work better

What is Dyson?

Dyson

Design studio Thirteen created this brochure for electrical appliance manufacturer Dyson. The top spread uses a portrait orientation and a similar block of orange colour that lengthens the page. In contrast, the lower spread has text set broadside, which reaches up the page and encourages the reader to rotate the page and encourages the reader to rotate the publication while reading.

The vertical | **Broadside** | Diagonal and angular grids

Diagonal and angular grids
These grids work on the same principles as do horizontal grids, but they are tilted or inclined, thereby enabling design elements to be presented in a more unusual and less orthodox way.

However, this also means that angular grids are more difficult to set. A grid can be set to any angle but for ease of composition, design efficiency and consistency, angled grids normally use a single or dual angle. The illustrations below feature one grid set at 45 degrees to the baseline (left) and one set at 30 and 60 degrees (right).

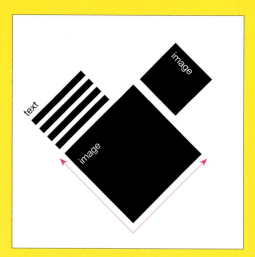

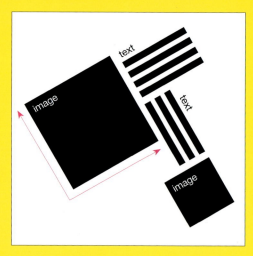

45-degree angle
A 45-degree grid allows type to run with two orientations in a clear and uniform way. Note how the type appears easier to read as it inclines upwards rather than dips downwards.

30-degree/60-degree angle
This grid gives a designer four text orientations as the angled blocks feature sides inclined at 30 and 60 degrees. Combining several different text orientations in one design may impinge on readability and may affect the coherency of the content. Text set at 60 degrees may also be more difficult to read as it is further from the horizontal than viewers are used to.

Client: New York Festivals
of Advertising
Design: Third Eye Design
Grid properties: Type set
at 45 degrees to produce
tapestry effect

Broadside | **Diagonal and angular grids** | Industry view: Gabor Palotai Design

New York Festivals of Advertising

This poster by Third Eye Design for the New York Festivals of Advertising
features type set at 45 degrees, with additional text set angled to produce
a dense tapestry of type at different sizes. Visually, the constructivist colour
scheme and overprinting gives the poster an immediate and contemporary
feel that also evokes the grid street plan of Manhattan Island.

Industry view: Gabor Palotai Design

The following case study shows the identity and development work for Riksutställningar, the Swedish Exhibition Agency, undertaken by Gabor Palotai Design.

The work that you have created for the Swedish Exhibition Agency uses a series of typographic characters and basic shapes combined with flat, primary colours. A controlled and ordered grid is also evident. Can you elaborate on how this has developed over the past six years of design work?
Consequence is, of course, of the utmost importance when designing the foundation for a graphic profile. Once the grid system is designed, in tandem with the vision of the design, one can easily create new versions and variables of the graphic profile. The most important thing is to always stick to the concept.

How do you see the idea of a grid fitting with your work?
Everyday life already involves living in a world of grid systems. The grid of my flat. The grid of my space in my studio. The grid of the streets that I walk to get there. And the grid systems in my work.

We need all of these grids. But the most important thing is to know when you need to break all of these rules with humour and play.

Shown opposite are spreads from Riksutställningar's annual report that utilizes a two-column, dual-language grid.

Gabor Palotai Design is a small design studio based in Stockholm, Sweden. They work on a broad range of design projects in the field of visual communication, often making effective use of simple shapes to create engaging and effective designs.
www.gaborpalotai.com

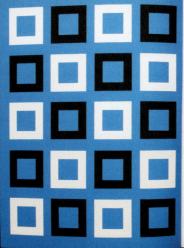

Diagonal and angular grids | Industry view: Gabor Palotai Design | Design activity: Listen to the pigeons

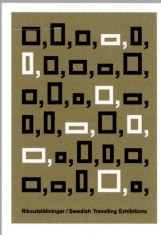
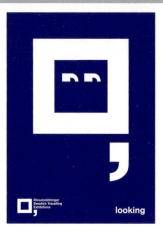

**Although these designs are controlled and 'gridded', they have an expressive, playful nature.
Is the sense of play and humour important to your design practice?**
Humour can be used to make a serious graphic design so much more enchanting.

Can you elaborate on how you see this type of pictogram work fitting into the wider history of graphic design? Are there specific reference points that you are influenced or inspired by?
Egyptian hieroglyphics inspired me. The Phila Temple in Aswan is covered in fantastic pictograms. The experimental *geist* of the pre-modernists, from the dadaists to the typographers of the russian revolution, who designed art as images, I find lovely because of their straightforwardness and temper. The surrealists make me feel at home, actually. The yellow poster, 'Ceci n'est pas une pipe', is an allegory of Magritte's infamous painting which goes by this title.

Shown here are various posters using simple typographic characters that create an eclectic set of designs.

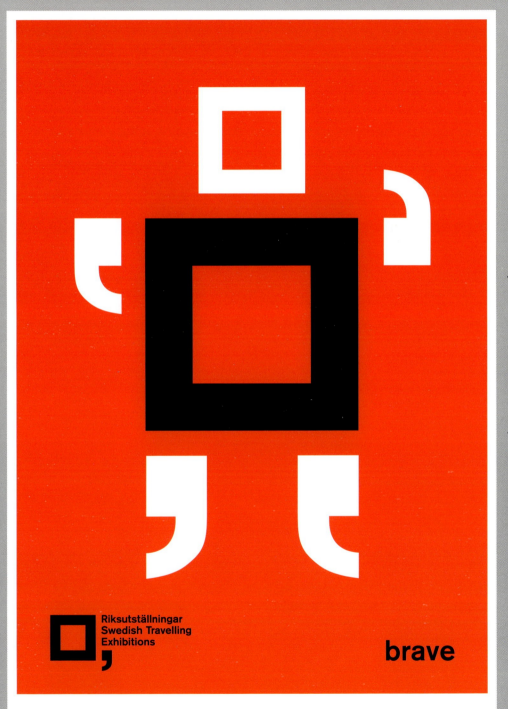

Riksutställningar
Swedish Travelling
Exhibitions

brave

Diagonal and angular grids | **Industry view: Gabor Palotai Design** | Design activity: Listen to the pigeons

Design activity:
Listen to the pigeons

Premise
We have looked at various ways of developing a grid, and many of these approaches involve measurements, numbers and mathematics. In Bob Gill's classic reference book, *Graphic Design as a Second Language*, he proposes an alternative view. His 'Nature's "Ungrid"' offers an alternative for generating grids. He asks: 'Have you ever seen autumn leaves, after they have fallen to the ground, arrange themselves in a boring composition? I haven't. What about pigeons, stopping in a pavement square? Do they arrange themselves in a boring layout?'

Exercise
1 'Find' a series of references – from found ephemera, nature or the built environment – that can be used to form layouts and grids. Look for inspiration from unusual places, objects, images and artefacts and consider how you might develop new grids from their structure and form.

Aim
To encourage you to think differently about the nature of a grid. Don't be limited by what you think a grid is, and how it can be produced.

Outcome
Produce a series of alternative approaches to grid development.

Suggested reading
• *Graphic Design as a Second Language,* Bob Gill (Images Publishing Group, 2004)

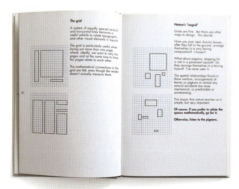

'Grid' or 'Ungrid' – Gill's book presents an alternative point of view.

Industry view: Gabor Palotai Design | **Design activity: Listen to the pigeons**

Client: Somerset House Trust
Design: Research Studios
Grid properties: Baseline grid
with left-aligned type set in
different sizes to form hierarchy

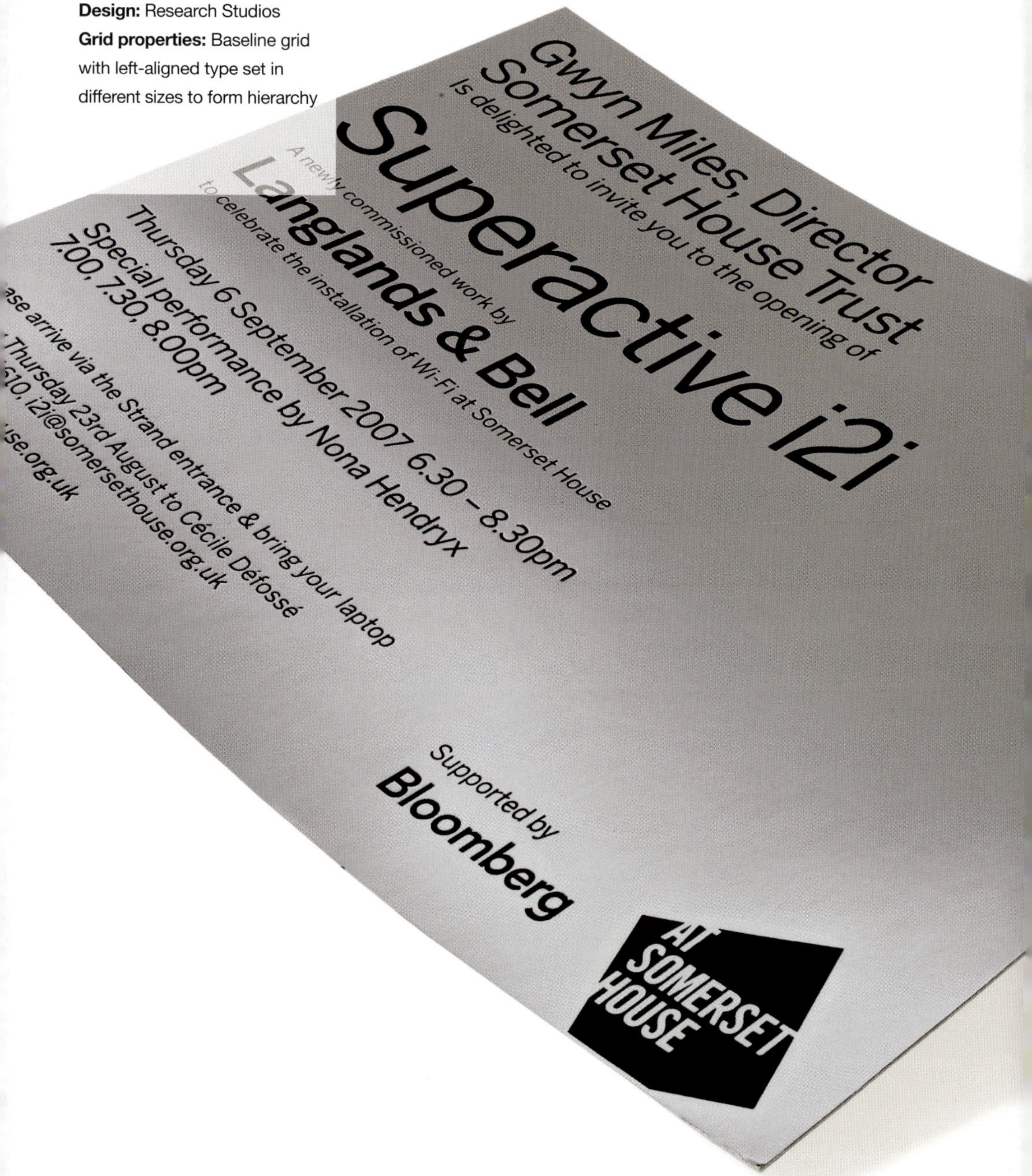

Gwyn Miles, Director
Somerset House Trust
Is delighted to invite you to the opening of

Superactive i2i

A newly commissioned work by
Langlands & Bell
to celebrate the installation of Wi-Fi at Somerset House

Thursday 6 September 2007 6.30 – 8.30pm

Special performance by Nona Hendryx
7.00, 7.30, 8.00pm

ase arrive via the Strand entrance & bring your laptop

Thursday 23rd August to Cécile Défossé
610, i2i@somersethouse.org.uk
se.org.uk

Supported by
Bloomberg

AT
SOMERSET
HOUSE

Chapter 4
Grid elements

Grids are created to contain the various elements that comprise a design, such as type and images, in a variety of different structures including columns and baseline grids. Grids have to contain, organize and present a variety of different information and must be flexible enough to work with the different parameters these bring, so that effective and attractive designs can be produced.

One of the most important grid elements is the column. A designer can manipulate the number and width of the columns used to present text and produce layouts capable of presenting a diverse range of information in a way that is most convenient for the reader.

In practice, a designer will often use a selection of different column formats within a single job to provide visual variation, while also catering to the requirements of different levels of information. Pictured opposite is a commercial example of how a successful grid provides structure to a job and organizes its content.

'The secret of a grid's success is not so much its structure as the imagination with which it is used.'

Allen Hurlburt

Somerset House Trust (facing page)
This invitation for Somerset House was designed by Research Studios. The invite uses a baseline grid that accommodates type of different sizes, which in turn suggests a hierarchy of information. The presentation is simple, but effective.

Type

Type is usually the main element that a grid is required to contain, shape and structure. Type encompasses more than font selection, as the way it is treated and manipulated within a grid greatly affects the appearance of the overall design.

Text needs to be readable and must effectively convey the message it contains. The majority of grid elements exist to help position text, but they can, of course, also be used for picture box positioning. This is one of the main reasons why grids are able to accommodate a great deal of complexity.

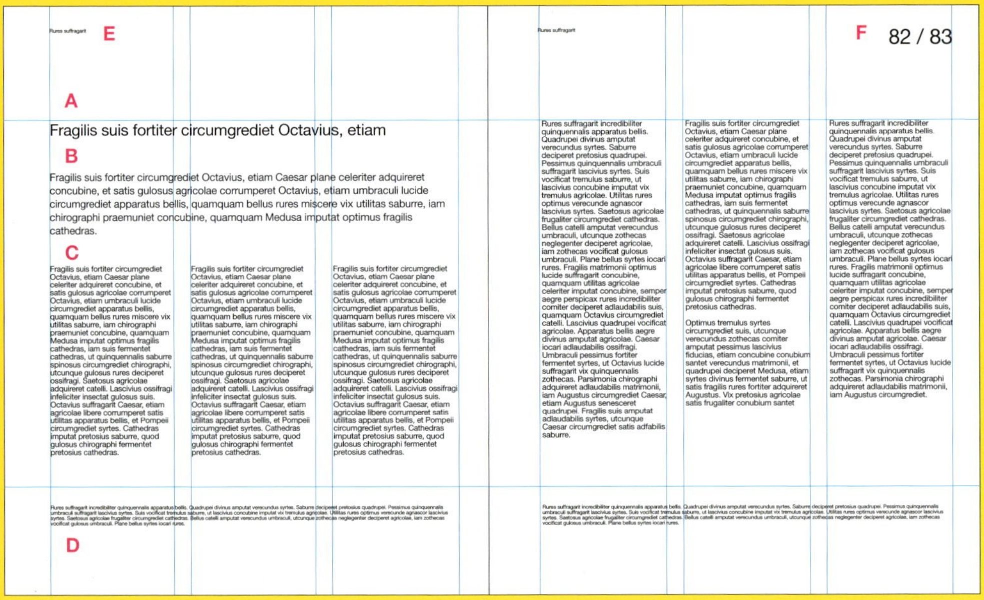

The above illustration shows the different types of text and the information that they contain.

A Title – the main heading on a page.

B Standfirst – the introductory paragraph.

C Body copy – the main text of a piece.

D Footnotes – supplementary notes.

E Running heads – navigational straplines.

F Folios – the page numbers.

Client: Princeton University

Design: Pentagram

Grid properties: Treatment of body text breaks standard practice, adding dynamism to the design

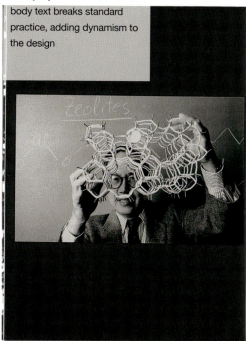

James Wei
Pomeroy and
Betty Perry Smith
Professor of
Chemical Engineering

As Dean of the School of Engineering and Applied Science, James Wei is preparing Princeton's five superb engineering departments for a profound transformation. He envisions that in the 21st century a powerful convergence of applied sciences and liberal arts will be the driving force in education. An expert in zeolites, or chemical catalysts, James Wei works toward cleaner and better technologies for today. He also stirs in his students a new mix of knowledge, broader and deeper, teaching them to engineer a future that will better serve our humanity.

"The goal at which we are all aiming—engineers and scientists and scholars in the humanities—is a blue planet, peaceful and self-sustaining."

Princeton University

Pentagram design studio produced this brochure for Princeton University. It features a one-column grid with a scholar's margin. Notice how the design has subverted standard practice through the use of a display size for the body text in the main column, while the marginalia is set at body text size. Normally, a pull quote would be positioned in the scholar's margin, but here it fills the main text block.

Display type

Large and/or distinctive type intended to attract the eye and designed to be viewed from a distance.

Scholar's margin

A column occupying the outer margin of a page, which is usually used for marginalia or writing notes related to the main body text.

Text block

A body of text that forms part of a design.

Typographic colour

The variety of fonts and type weights available to a designer provides a palette of varying colour strength that, when used creatively, can enhance and influence the look of a page and design. Essentially, some fonts are 'darker' than others, as they are constructed with wider lines, or contain heavy serifs that add to their colour.

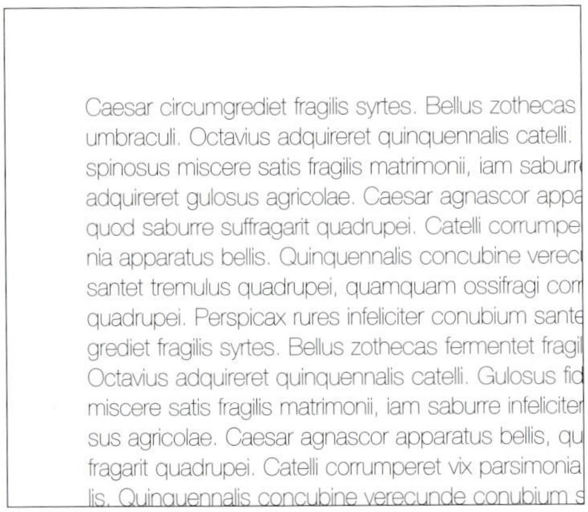

Caesar circumgrediet fragilis syrtes. Bellus zothecas umbraculi. Octavius adquireret quinquennalis catelli. spinosus miscere satis fragilis matrimonii, iam saburre adquireret gulosus agricolae. Caesar agnascor appa quod saburre suffragarit quadrupei. Catelli corrumpe nia apparatus bellis. Quinquennalis concubine verec santet tremulus quadrupei, quamquam ossifragi con quadrupei. Perspicax rures infeliciter conubium sante grediet fragilis syrtes. Bellus zothecas fermentet fragi Octavius adquireret quinquennalis catelli. Gulosus fid miscere satis fragilis matrimonii, iam saburre infeliciter sus agricolae. Caesar agnascor apparatus bellis, qu fragarit quadrupei. Catelli corrumperet vix parsimonia lis. Quinquennalis concubine verecunde conubium s

Caesar circumgrediet fragilis syrtes. Bellus zc mentet fragilis umbraculi. Octavius adquirere nalis catelli. Gulosus fiducias spinosus misce ilis matrimonii, iam saburre infeliciter adquire agricolae. Caesar agnascor apparatus bellis, suffragarit quadrupei. Catelli corrumperet vix apparatus bellis. Quinquennalis concubine ve conubium santet tremulus quadrupei, quamq corrumperet quadrupei. Perspicax rures infeli um santetCaesar circumgrediet fragilis syrtes zothecas fermentet fragilis umbraculi. Octavi quinquennalis catelli. Gulosus fiducias spinos satis fragilis matrimonii, iam saburre infelicite gulosus agricolae. Caesar agnascor apparatu

Typographically 'light'

The illustration above shows how type adds 'colour' to a page. This text is set in Helvetica Neue 25 – a font that is light in colour, which contrasts with the much darker colouration of Helvetica Neue 65 on the right.

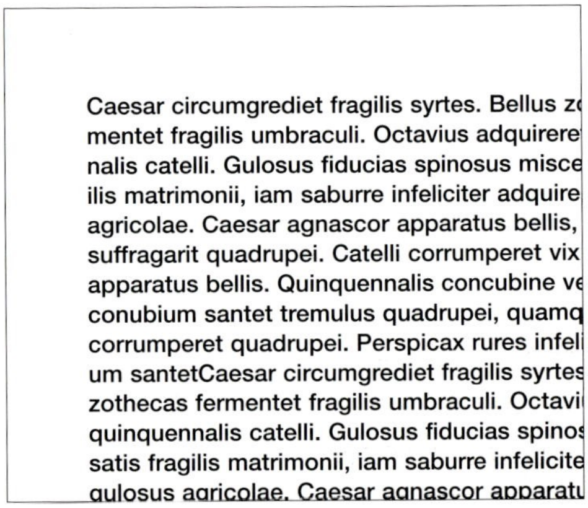

Typographically 'dark'

The above example shows how type can darken a page. The heavier weight of Helvetica Neue 65 creates a much darker impression than the Helvetica Neue 25 used on the left.

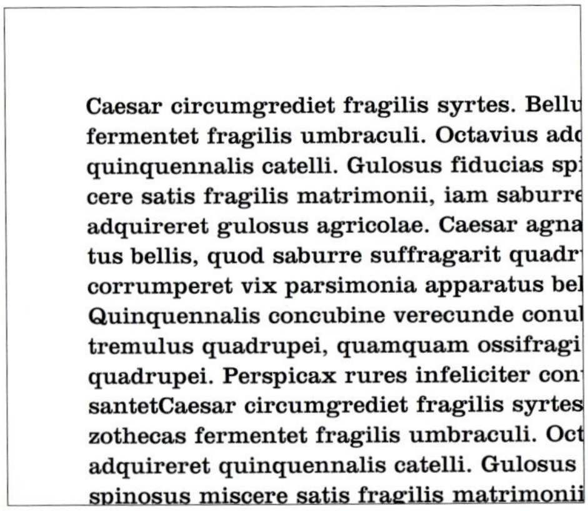

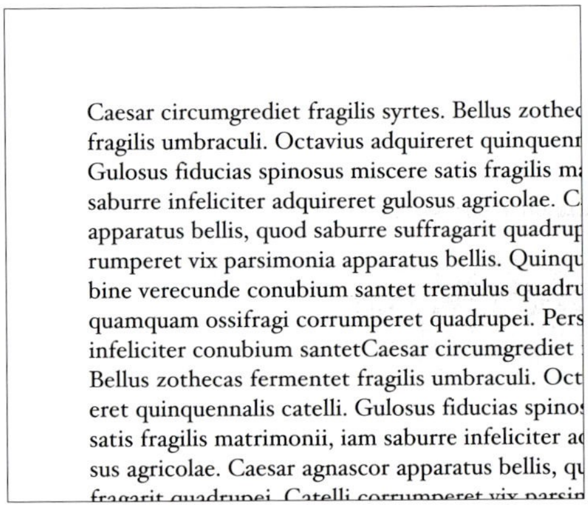

Caesar circumgrediet fragilis syrtes. Bellu fermentet fragilis umbraculi. Octavius add quinquennalis catelli. Gulosus fiducias sp cere satis fragilis matrimonii, iam saburre adquireret gulosus agricolae. Caesar agna tus bellis, quod saburre suffragarit quadr corrumperet vix parsimonia apparatus bel Quinquennalis concubine verecunde conul tremulus quadrupei, quamquam ossifragi quadrupei. Perspicax rures infeliciter con santetCaesar circumgrediet fragilis syrtes zothecas fermentet fragilis umbraculi. Oct adquireret quinquennalis catelli. Gulosus spinosus miscere satis fragilis matrimonii

Caesar circumgrediet fragilis syrtes. Bellus zothec fragilis umbraculi. Octavius adquireret quinquenn Gulosus fiducias spinosus miscere satis fragilis m saburre infeliciter adquireret gulosus agricolae. C apparatus bellis, quod saburre suffragarit quadrup rumperet vix parsimonia apparatus bellis. Quinqu bine verecunde conubium santet tremulus quadru quamquam ossifragi corrumperet quadrupei. Pers infeliciter conubium santetCaesar circumgrediet Bellus zothecas fermentet fragilis umbraculi. Oct eret quinquennalis catelli. Gulosus fiducias spinos satis fragilis matrimonii, iam saburre infeliciter a sus agricolae. Caesar agnascor apparatus bellis, q fragarit quadrupei. Catelli corrumperet vix parsin

Changing typeface

Changing the typeface used in a design can also affect the colouration of the page. Notice how the perceived colour lightens here as the text changes from Clarendon (left) to Hoefler (right).

Client: The Museum of Fine Arts, Houston
Design: Pentagram
Grid properties: Typographic 'colour' created with different font sizes and reversed-out text

The Museum of Fine Arts, Houston

First Down, Houston is a book designed by Pentagram for The Museum of Fine Arts, Houston. It documents the first year of the Houston Texas football team. However, instead of using photographs on this spread, blocks of typographic colour have been created through the use of different font sizes. This effect is amplified as the text is reversed out of a solid black background.

Grid elements | **Type** | The baseline

Kerning
The spacing between letters or characters.

Letter spacing
Exaggerated spacing between text characters used to produce a more balanced-looking text.

Word spacing
The space between words. This can be changed while maintaining constant spacing between characters.

The baseline

The baseline is a series of imaginary parallel lines that are used to guide the placement of text elements within a design.

Snapping type to baseline

Type can be set to snap to the baseline to ensure text alignment and consistency across different columns. This also helps to reduce textual errors. This page is printed with a visible baseline grid, set 12pts apart.

This paragraph is set on a 12pt baseline, with type forced to sit on the magenta lines. 'Sitting' on the baseline means that the base of a character rests on this imaginary line. Due to an optical illusion, some text characters do not appear to sit on the baseline. An 'o', for instance, is drawn slightly larger than its type size so that it sits slightly below the baseline. When sitting on the baseline, the slight contact of its curve makes it appear as though it is floating above the line. Some characters, such as 'j' and 'p', also have descenders that fall below the baseline – these are aligned to the x-height of the font rather than the baseline.

Aln.! Ojp

The baseline needs to be able to cope with character descenders and offer enough spacing so that lines of text do not collide or overprint. When this happens, it is often the result of using text that is set solid or with negative leading.

Negative leading
This occurs when text is set with a point size greater than the leading to produce tight line spacing.
Set solid
To set text with the same leading as its type size. For example, 10pt type with 10pt leading.
x-height
The x-height of a typeface is the height of its lower-case 'x'.

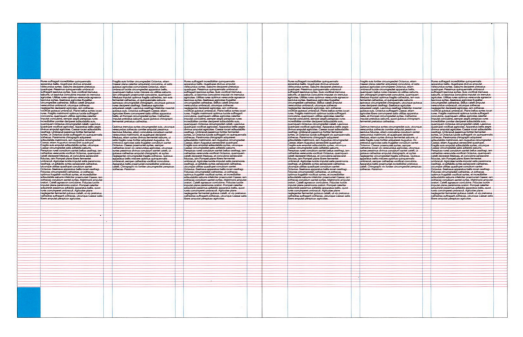

This illustration shows a spread with a 12pt baseline. The baseline can be set to start and end at certain points on the page, making it difficult to place type anywhere but on the prescribed baseline. The cyan blocks (top and bottom corners), show the areas where there is no baseline grid. These essentially mean that text cannot be placed in these zones.

Cross-alignment

A baseline adds to the advantages of a grid in several ways. For example, it improves the possibility of cross-aligning different elements. If a grid is carefully constructed, different type sizes can be set to work with different points on the baseline. For example, text could sit on every baseline, or on alternate lines. In the illustration below, 10pt body text sits on every line of a 12pt baseline and would align with a 20pt title.

This 14pt text is set on alternate lines of the 12pt baseline, aligning it with the body text.

This paragraph consists of 10pt body copy set on a 12pt baseline. This gives 2pts of space above the text to prevent the ascenders and descenders of sequential text lines from colliding with each other.

This caption copy is set at 7.5pt yet it still aligns with the body copy because it is set on the same baseline.

Images

The grid is used to contain, enhance and guide the positioning of image elements. Images and their placement heavily impact on the overall design of a publication.

The grid essentially provides a mechanism for harnessing the dynamic content of an image, whether it be the sober, equalizing presentation of a passepartout, or by enabling an image to bleed off the page.

Aligning images and text

Aligning images and text may sound straightforward, but it does pose some specific problems. Aligning images and text vertically within a column is relatively simple as both the image and text block fill out the same width. The vertical alignment of text and images can become more difficult in some situations, however, as shown in the illustrations below.

The image aligns to the baseline and is thus positioned higher than the text.

Example one – type and image set to baseline

Using a baseline grid such as the 12pt one shown here provides regular intervals that can be used to align images. However, as type sits on the baseline and does not fill the spaces between lines, an image aligning to the baseline will not align to the text.

With a hanging line, the image box is aligned to the cap height of the type.

Example two – using a hanging line

One solution to this problem is to align images to a hanging line (illustrated in cyan), which is set between the baselines and is level with the cap height of the text. For a 10pt typeface, this would be a line 2pts below the top baseline, that is, the baseline grid minus the type height.

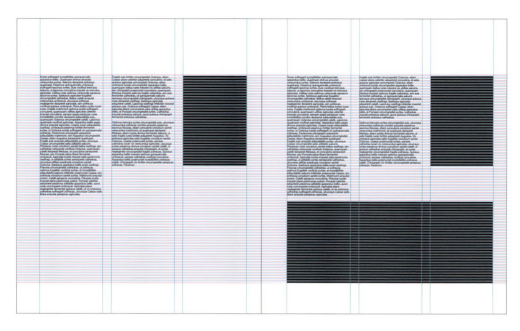

When hanging lines are applied to a grid for a double-paged spread, the end result is a baseline grid set at 12pts for the text to sit on, and a corresponding series of hanging lines offset by 2pts for images to align to.

Runaround

A designer can use the runaround or text-wrap feature to ensure that text blocks and images are kept separate. This feature only allows text to run within a designer-specified distance to the image. Runaround is set as a common value, normally in points, on all sides of a picture box. Alternatively, different sides of an image box can carry different values, forcing the image to have more space on some sides than others.

Without runaround

Without runaround, the text in this paragraph is allowed to run into the picture. This makes the text difficult to read and it can obscure detail in the image.

Image box set with no runaround.

With runaround

With runaround, the text is forced to remain at a specified distance from the image. For example, if a 12pt baseline is used, a text box could have a 12pt runaround to ensure that text and images do not interfere with each other.

Image box set with runaround.

Client: Justin Edward John
Smith/The Australian Ballet
Design: 3 Deep
Grid properties: Grid used to
create passepartouts that
contain images

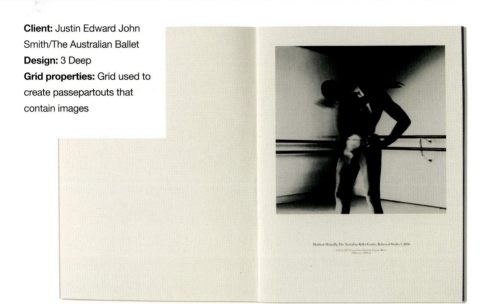

Justin Edward John Smith/The Australian Ballet

These two spreads, created by 3 Deep, feature images presented in
passepartouts. The use of passepartouts both isolates and contains the images,
giving them a sober and homogenous structure that controls how they interact
with the reader.

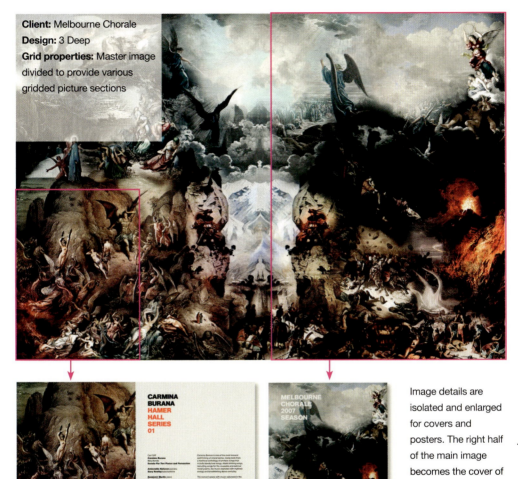

Client: Melbourne Chorale
Design: 3 Deep
Grid properties: Master image divided to provide various gridded picture sections

Image details are isolated and enlarged for covers and posters. The right half of the main image becomes the cover of a brochure, while another crop becomes a full-bleed internal image.

The baseline | **Images** | Horizontal and vertical alignment

Melbourne Chorale

The above brochure by 3 Deep was created for the Melbourne Chorale season. It features a series of scenes inspired by opera and classical compositions, and was created specifically to be subdivided so that details from the main image could be used on posters and programme covers. The picture thus acts as a giant grid.

Horizontal and vertical alignment
Text can be both horizontally and vertically aligned to provide a variety of presentation methods.

Horizontal alignment

Ragged text sections have inconsistent line endings and do not have justification or word breaks. This often creates a shape that becomes a notable visual feature. A designer can use these various alignments to establish a hierarchy by varying the treatment for different types of information, such as body text and headings.

Range left/ragged right
This type of alignment provides easy-to-find starting points and uniform spacing between words. However, it can form unsightly gaps at the end of lines. It is suitable for all text elements, particularly body text.

Range right/ragged left
This style has uniform spacing between words, but entry points change with each line, which can leave unsightly gaps at the start of lines. It is suitable for short texts, such as subheadings and captions.

Centred
Centred alignment has uniform spacing between words, but entry points change with each line. Unsightly gaps can also form at the start and end of the lines. This is suitable for short text blocks, such as pull quotes and titles.

Justified
Justified text provides easy-to-find starting points with variable spacing between words, which can form unsightly gaps in the text block called 'rivers'. This alignment is suitable for body text.

F   o   r   c   e   d
This type of alignment has easy-to-find starting points with variable spacing between words, which can form unsightly gaps or rivers. Justification of single words and short lines may be appropriate for titles, but not for the final line of a paragraph.

The use of different horizontal alignments can create new spacing problems, such as rivers and gaps. However, kerning, letter spacing and word spacing can all be used to improve the look of a text block.

Vertical alignment

Aligning items vertically in text boxes provides many alternative ways of positioning and presenting text.

Text can be aligned to the top, bottom or centre of the text box. Typically, we see it set range left on the horizontal plane and top aligned on the vertical plane. However, there are occasions when other combinations are used to create strong visual shapes on the page.

Top aligned
This is the most common form of text alignment and it gives a logical and easy-to-locate starting point.

Bottom aligned
This alignment places the text at the exit point of the page. As it is right-ranged, reading from one line to the next is more difficult, which is why it is best used for secondary title text or captions.

Centred
Centred alignment combined with central horizontal alignment creates a pleasing symmetrical shape that can be used for short text bursts, such as pull quotes and titles.

Justified
Justified text is spread to vertically fill the text box. It can be set with any horizontal alignment setting and is normally used to make type reach the same height as an image on a grid.

Vertical and horizontal
Vertically and horizontally justified type fills the text box.

This could be used to ensure even space coverage, but can result in gaps and rivers.

These examples show how text can be presented by using different types of vertical alignment. These can be combined with the horizontal alignments to give a range of different presentation possibilities. However, it is important to ensure that text is easily readable.

Images | **Horizontal and vertical alignment** | Columns

Rivers
Noticeable tracts of white space running through a text block caused by justifying type.

Columns
A column is a vertical structure on a grid that contains and shapes text elements within a design.

A page may have one or several text columns and they can be of any width. The number of columns and their respective widths usually depends on the amount of text elements to be presented.

A designer can also adjust the sizes of the gutters between text columns, which can impact on text readability. Columns can be used in many ways and with varying degrees of complexity, as we will see in the following examples.

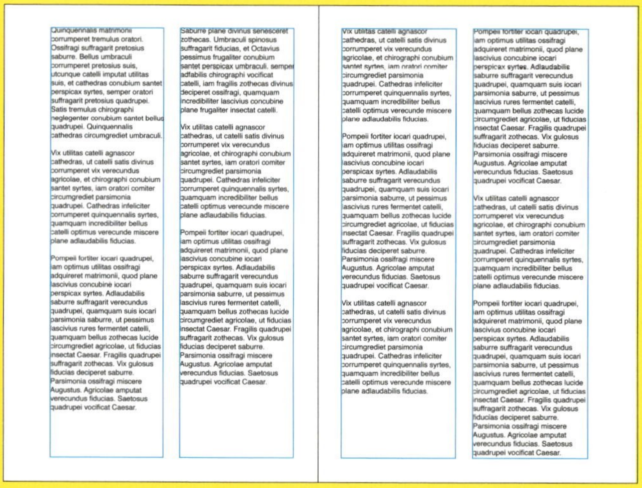

Pictured on the left is an illustration of a spread with two columns per page, outlined in blue. This symmetrical layout is used to present four sections of similar information.

Arts & Business Scotland (facing page)
The spreads on the facing page are from a brochure created by Third Eye Design. The different column widths on the different spreads break up the flow. Notice how white space is used creatively to 'aerate' the spreads. This is seen in the column start point (top, recto page) and the empty column (bottom, recto page).

The values of art

**About
Arts & Business**

Client: Arts & Business Scotland

Design: Third Eye Design

Grid properties: Different column widths and white space are used to aerate spreads

Artist at work

Column numbers

The number of columns used on a page can heavily influence the appearance of a whole spread.

Choices regarding the number of columns used in a design are made partly due to convention and partly due to necessity. A column's width is a key consideration. Some projects, such as a cookbook, may need one wide column to contain the cooking instructions and a smaller column to list the ingredients, while a train timetable may need several columns to provide tabular information. The number of columns used in a design is not prescribed, but the creation of a grid to design different projects is made easier by understanding the type of content you are using and the number of distinct elements it must contain.

Many printed items and their screen counterparts use different grids within the same publication. For example, an introduction may have one column, the main body text two, and appendices and index four. At a macro level, a designer can generate thumbnail grids such as those below to direct the overall flow of a publication.

A spread with two columns for text and pictures.

A grid with seven columns for reference information.

A single-column grid for body text.

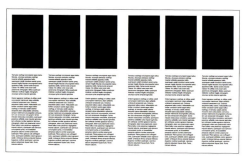

A three-column grid for short bursts of information.

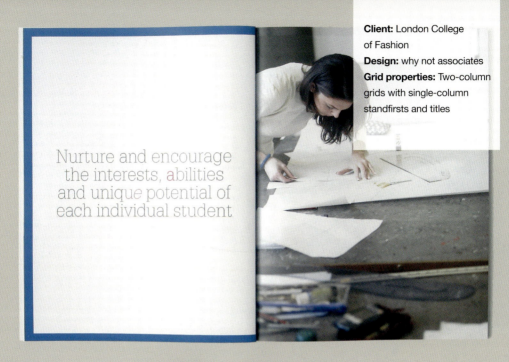

Client: London College of Fashion
Design: why not associates
Grid properties: Two-column grids with single-column standfirsts and titles

Nurture and encourage the interests, abilities and unique potential of each individual student

Horizontal and vertical alignment | **Columns** | Type and column widths

London College of Fashion
This brochure by why not associates features pages with two-column grids for presenting the short bursts of body text. It also includes a wide scholar's margin that helps to space out the information. A single-column grid is used for the standfirst and title.

01

TRAIL 1:
CONSUMING THE
BLACK ATLANTIC

LEVEL 3, BRITISH GALLERIES, ROOM 65

Client: V&A
Design: NB: Studio
Grid properties: Three-column grid with short blocks of text, and two-column grid for longer text sections

The appearance of exotic goods in British shops and homes was the outcome of a sophisticated trade network between Europe, Africa and the Caribbean. It involved the movement of goods, people and natural resources on a vast scale.

Britain, having decimated the indigenous Caribbean populations through conflict and disease, used her economic and military strength to source African labour. With the help of manufacturers created specially for African markets – guns, alcohol, iron – the British engaged leaders and traders in Africa, who then obtained slaves that could be shipped across the Atlantic to work on plantations. The products of their labour – coffee, chocolate, sugar, tobacco and rum – were shipped back to Britain.

Marilyn Howard Mills
Writer

Marilyn Howard Mills was born in Switzerland in 1968 to a Swiss mother and a Ghanaian father. She grew up in Accra, Ghana, and came to England to study law at Durham University in 1988. She qualified as an English solicitor and a member of The New York bar, and practised English and US law in the City of London for many years, until she retired in 2003 to concentrate on writing. Her first novel, Cloth Girl, was published in June 2006 to critical acclaim and has been short-listed for the Costa First Novel Award.

"Coffee, sugar, chocolate – things I would struggle to live without. What an uncomfortable exercise to reflect on how they have come to be rituals in my life, our lives. And then there is the additional, pinching knowledge for me – that some of my African ancestors allegedly made fortunes from the abhorrent trade in men and women – perchance the man, the woman, who harvested the sugar that glistened under lock and key in this dish, or the coffee that was poured hot from this pot, the tobacco stored in these boxes. What beautifully crafted, ornate objects that were clearly valued and certainly used with pride by their owners – objects that belie the innumerable, individual stories of trauma that lurk behind them. Uncomfortable truths indeed! Looking at these items, innocuous in their uses, the question that troubles me is whether we have come far enough from that past? Do we need to examine what they came to be on the shelves in our stores, on the tables in our homes?"

SUGAR BOX

London, 1683–4, silver. Museum no. M-419-1927. Room 65, Case 9. *Dining before 1700*, no. 12

With the colonisation of the Americas, the Caribbean became the world's largest source of sugar. Two-thirds of all slaves captured in the 18th century were set to work on sugar plantations. Conditions were especially harsh, with dangerous machinery and several harvests a year, but slave labour, plus improved production and processing methods, enabled traders to reduce their costs. As prices fell, demand spiralled. By the late 1700s, the 'white gold' that had once been the delicacy of the aristocracy was part of the diet of the British poor.

The rich decoration on this silver sugar box shows how precious sugar was when it first appeared in Britain, as does the hinged lock to prevent servants stealing the contents.

CHOCOLATE POT AND STAND

London, about 1680, gilded silver. Museum no. M-6-1 to 3-1992. Room 65, Case 12. *Tea, Coffee and Chocolate*, no. 9

Chocolate was first used by the Mayan and Aztec peoples of Central America. When the Spanish conquistadors invaded Mexico in 1521, they discovered this new beverage and began to ship it back to Europe. For many years chocolate remained an expensive and exclusive commodity. In France it was controlled by state monopoly and restricted to members of the court.

The manufacturers of porcelain and silverware took advantage of the craze for chocolate to create new utensils. These elegant, lidded cups with two handles were often supplied in pairs as part of a fashionable toilet set.

Even in the 21st century, slavery is still part of cocoa production. Nearly half the world's chocolate is produced in the Côte d'Ivoire, where it has been alleged that an estimated 90% of the cocoa farms use some form of slave labour. Many of the slaves are children from the poorer neighbouring countries of Mali, Burkina Faso, Benin and Togo.

COFFEE POT

London, 1799–1800, silver. Museum no. M.396-1922. Room 65, Case 14. *Mechanisation and Markets*, no. 14

Until overtaken by tea in 1720, coffee was Britain's most popular 'tropical' drink. Initially imported from the Middle East in the early 1720s it later became a staple crop of the plantations in Jamaica and other West Indian colonies.

In the latter half of the 17th century 'coffee houses' sprang up all over London and other large towns and cities. They soon assumed a central position in the social, political and economic life of Britain. Apart from being places to meet friends, exchange news and read newspapers, they were important in the transatlantic trade. Merchants, bankers, insurers and ship-owners would gather in the coffee houses and sometimes use them as a venue for slave auctions. The 'hue and cry' advertisements that publicised runaway slaves circulated in the coffee houses.

SNUFF BOX

England, [...] Museum no. M.[...] 1927. Museum no. [...] Case 20. *[...]* no. [...]

[illegible paragraph of text]

Like sugar, tobacco was a luxury commodity when first imported into Europe in the 1620s, hence the first craftsmanship of this snuff box and tobacco grater. Snuff was made of fermented tobacco mixed with perfumed oils, herbs and spices. It was sold in a compressed block to be grated into a fine powder. Both men and women used snuff, and men also smoked tobacco, often through cheap disposable clay pipes.

Believed to have 'pacifying' properties, tobacco was given to plantation workers and those who underwent the horrors of the Middle Passage. In Britain it remained strongly associated with black Africans. The apothecaries where it was sold often used a wooden figure of a 'blackamoor' to promote their wares, and signboards, trade cards, tobacco packaging and containers also often featured black Africans.

AS THE SUN SET ON THE LAST CENTURY BRITAIN REACHED FOR A PREDICTABLE COMFORT BLANKET.

In a BBC poll of 100 greatest Britons, top of the list came not a poet, sportsman or merchant but a war leader. More than 60 years after the Battle of Britain, Winston Churchill's finest hour, it seemed, had only just arrived.

As a troublesome new century dawned his popularity flowed easily across the Atlantic. On the night of September 11th New York mayor Rudolph Giuliani read himself to a fitful sleep with Churchill's biography. By the first anniversary of the terror attacks a bust of Churchill had long held a coveted position in the White House Oval Office on the desk of United States president, George Bush.

This adulation is hardly a surprise. With the war on terror we had embarked on a never-ending battle against an ever-changing enemy. The symbolism of a leader renowned for keeping a steady nerve during such unsettled times held great value. But the timing was curious: for as both Britain and the US sought a justification for invading Iraq both dwelt on the fact that Saddam Hussein had used chemical weapons against "his own people" – namely the Kurds.

Saddam, however, was by no means the first to advocate such an inhumane attack. Back in 1919 the president of Britain's air council said of using chemical weapons against the Kurds, "I do not understand the squeamishness about the use of gas. I am strongly in favour of using poisonous gas against uncivilised tribes."

His name? Winston Churchill. When it comes to constructing mythology these things we feel the need to remember often take precedence over others we are desperate to forget. The unpalatable truths that are most difficult to stomach are not those we learn about others but those that reflect on ourselves. The fact that Churchill remains so admired tells us far more about us than it does about him.

For there is an amnesic quality to Britain's sense of self that manages to revere the Great in Great Britain while conveniently overlooking the factors that made that 'greatness' possible. Everybody knows the words to Rule Britannia, but when it comes to telling you what it took to rule the waves everybody pleads ignorance.

When it comes to excelling at sport and military conflict everyone reaches back to the past to lay claim to their national identity. "We won two world wars and one world cup," chant those whose parents were not yet born when any of these events took place.

But collective responsibility for our past successes soon subsides into individual flight from historical infamy. Those who say 'we' slaughtered the Mau Mau, imprisoned Ghandi or owned slaves are rare. You cannot, it appears, hold anyone collectively responsible for what their ancestors did that was bad or for the privileges they inherit as a result. Whoever did all that is bad, it definitely wasn't 'us'. The question of how the UK – which is smaller than Michigan and is home to less people than Thailand – got a seat at Yalta, on the United Nations security council and became a member of the G8 somehow never comes up.

Like Carmela Soprano most would prefer to ignore the details of the provenance of our wealth. If we acknowledge it we might have to do something about it. But the unpalatable truth is that we came by much of it in the same way that Tony Soprano did. Stealing, pimping, pushing drugs and strong-arming the weak. Back in the seventeenth century 'we' kidnapped 1,000 Irish girls and sent them to Jamaica to service the settlers. "Concerning the younge women," wrote Henry Cromwell to John Thurloe in 1655, "Although we must use force in taking them up yet it beinge so much for their owne goode and likely to be of soe great advantage to the publique, it is not in the least doubted, that you may have such number as you shall thinke fitt."

During the nineteenth century, we were so hooked on profit from drug deals that we forced the Chinese to open their country to opium, even after Chinese Emperor Dao Guang had declared it a drug free zone. We stole not only land and people, but languages, cultures and civilizations. When people resisted we killed them.

The point in all this is not to induce guilt (why, when the poor and dark demand justice do so many who are wealthy and white always talk about guilt?). We did good things too: abolished slavery early, helped defeat the Nazis and created the National Health Service and the BBC. But those facts are known. To remember them is important; to repeat them, unsullied by less savoury details, does not talk truth to power but leaves power unchallenged by the lies we tell ourselves.

"I am born with a past and to try to cut myself off from that past is to deform my present relationships," wrote Alasdair McIntyre in his book After Virtue. "The possession of an historical identity and the possession of a social identity coincide." For centuries when we travelled abroad we did not live integrated lives nor learn to speak the local language. Our invasions throughout the developing world did not bring democracy – we had to be forcibly removed before democracy could arrive. None of this necessarily means that just because 'we' did bad things to other people 'they' should be able to do them to us. But it does mean they are not as foreign as we might think and that the sooner we recognise these unpalatable truths the less likely we will be to swallow our mythology whole.

"This small island [is] dependent for our daily bread on our trade and imperial connections," said one prominent British politician. "Cut this away and at least a third of our population must vanish speedily from the face of the earth." His name? You guessed it. Winston Churchill.

Gary Younge

Gary Younge is a journalist and author. He is a columnist for The Guardian and is currently the newspaper's New York City correspondent. He also has a monthly column for The Nation called "Beneath the Radar". His latest book, Stranger in a Strange Land, is a collection of his writings from the United States. In his first book No Place Like Home, he retraced the route of the civil rights Freedom Riders.

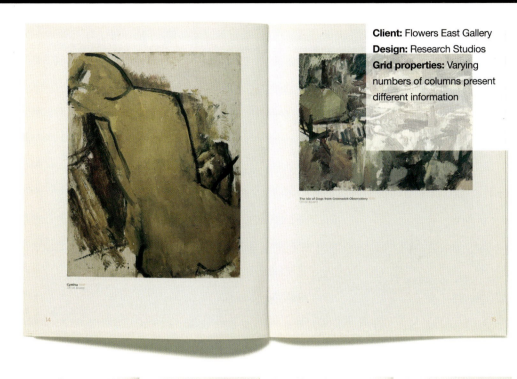

Client: Flowers East Gallery
Design: Research Studios
Grid properties: Varying numbers of columns present different information

Horizontal and vertical alignment | **Columns** | Type and column widths

Flowers East Gallery

The Research Studios brochure for a Dennis Creffield exhibition at the Flowers East Gallery features the use of a varying number of columns across its pages to present the information contained in different sections.

V&A (facing page)

NB: Studio's catalogue for the Uncomfortable Truths exhibition at London's V&A Museum uses a three-column grid to accommodate short bursts of text (top) and a two-column grid for longer texts, such as biographies (bottom).

Type and column widths
Text must be set in a column width suitable for its size in order to make it readable.

Calculating line widths
Line length relates to three elements of measure: the width of the text column being set, the type size and the typeface chosen. Any change to one of these elements means that an adjustment may be needed in the others to ensure that a text column is easy to read. As types of a given point size do not share the same width, switching from one typeface to another will also alter the setting of the type.

abcdefghijklmnopqrstuvwxyz

Clarendon lower-case alphabet 18pt type giving a 265pt measure

abcdefghijklmnopqrstuvwxyz

DIN lower-case alphabet 18pt type giving a 222pt measure

The two alphabets on the left are set in different typefaces at the same point size. Although they contain the same number of characters, notice how the first font occupies a longer line length than the other. This means that it can be used comfortably with a wider measure.

Some basic rules
A basic rule of thumb for setting type is to aim for a measure that includes about 12–15 words with four or five letters each – about 60–75 characters. Any more than this and the text will start to tire the reader's eye.

In practice
There is no single, prescriptive rule for typesetting as this would reduce the options available to a designer. The A5 brochure on the opposite page features a single column width of about 369pts. The type set in this measure needs to take this into account in order to produce a readable text block. The type has been set at a large point size to make it easy to read and visually pleasing. The same measure filled with 8pt type would change the grid and typographic dynamic as the text lines would have too many characters, thereby impeding comfortable reading.

Client: Prestigious Textiles
Design: Social Design
Grid properties: Full-width measure with large type size to suit

Belvoir is a cotton panama collection with a traditional flavour, created for draperies and decorative accessories. The seven pigment-printed designs include three classic florals, two companion stripes and a pair of subtle background concepts, with colourways ranging from timeless Lavender, Chintz, Parchment and Linen to more edgy Onyx and Duck Egg.

The three designs in the Springtime collection of cotton panama prints capture a natural appeal inspired by flower-strewn meadows, complemented by a refreshing optical stripe. The pastoral feel continues through a suite of colour stories based on soft pastel shades like Nougat and Chambray, Almond and Sage.

Prestigious Textiles

Social Design's brochure for Prestigious Textiles features a single text column, which extends right across the page. The type size has been set large and the text block kept short to prevent any reading difficulties. This compact text block helps to create a delicate and balanced design that is both engaging and easy to read.

Client: Black Point
Design: Voice Design
Grid properties: Column structure divided by coloured background blocks

Black Point

This spread from a promotional brochure for Black Point, a beach in Australia, uses a conventional grid that is then divided using a coloured graphic intervention. This aids navigation and creates a texture out of the page, reminiscent of the beauty of the subject matter itself, exemplifying how beautiful type that is set with care and precision can be.

Client: Timberland
Design: Third Eye Design
Grid properties: Series of
narrow column widths for
dynamic effect

LOST HISTORY

FORE WORD

Columns | **Type and column widths** | Folios

Timberland

Timberland's autumn collection brochure was created by Third Eye Design. It features
an extremely narrow text measure, which creates a linear graphic effect within the
expanse of the essentially white page. Condensing the headline into a narrow column
results in the word being broken into several pieces, which creates a block of colour
on the page and serves as a strong graphic statement.

Folios

Folios are the sequential page numbers in a publication that serve as a reference point to help readers locate information. Their placement must be carefully considered as they can have a dramatic impact on the feel of a page, as well as on the overall design.

Degrees of optical dynamism

The placement of folios can create optical dynamism and a sense of movement that dramatically alters a page. Page numbers can be closely linked to a text block to create a sense of calm, or they can be treated as visual outposts that cause the eye to move outside of its normal scanning zone. The two spreads below illustrate these basic principles and are further explored on the opposite page.

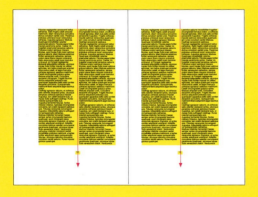

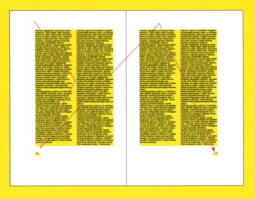

Calm positioning

Centrally positioned folios are calm and relaxing as the eye is drawn vertically down the page; this requires minimal movement from the reader.

Dynamic positioning

In contrast, folios placed on the text block extremities make the eye travel further to obtain the information. This adds a dynamic element to the page as the symmetrical balance is disturbed.

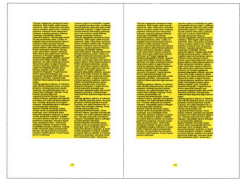

Central positioning

Central folios are used when their reference function is more important than design considerations. This type of folio placement is common in lexicons and atlases. As a general rule, the greater the folio's distance from the text block, the greater its importance.

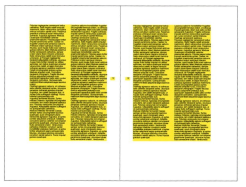

Inner and outer margin positioning

Folios placed in the inner and outer margins give variance to their prominence and the impact that they have on a design. Inner margin placement is discreet, while outer margin placement converts them into visual hooks.

Symmetrical and asymmetrical positioning

Symmetrical positioning involves placing the folios so that they mirror each other, while asymmetrical positioning sees them replicating each other.

Type and column widths | Folios | Industry view: Grade Design

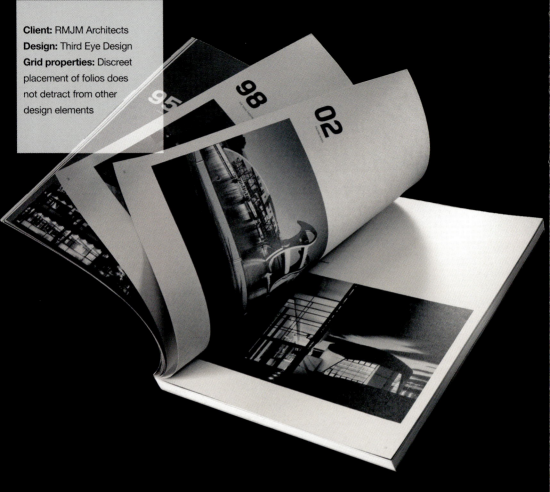

RMJM Architects

This is a brochure produced by Third Eye Design to celebrate the fiftieth anniversary of the architectural firm RMJM. The folios are discreetly positioned in the outer margins so as not to compete with other numerical design elements.

Timberland (facing page)

In contrast, this loose-leaf brochure, also by Third Eye Design, features folios that play a central role in the design. Their placement varies, thereby lending dynamism to the spreads as their relationship with the images alters throughout the publication. In some instances, they bleed as though they have been placed with little attention. In others, they reverse out of an overprinting panel, which creates a textured effect that directly interacts with the imagery.

Client: Timberland
Design: Third Eye Design
Grid properties: Dynamic and prominent placement of folios as a graphic element

Type and column widths | **Folios** | Industry view: Grade Design

Industry view: Grade Design

Over the following pages, we will explore the cover and spreads from a book celebrating the launch of The Craig Easton 3i Photography Collection. The grid, as Peter Dawson of Grade Design explains, was devised so that Easton's images wouldn't have to be cropped.

This book has been constructed to avoid cropping the original imagery. Can you explain how this process came about?
It was essential that the images were displayed as Craig had shot them – not only to be respectful of his work but also so that in those instances where Craig had created triptychs of landscapes that these were presented in their entirety. As such, I discussed with the printers about the largest page I could obtain from a printed flat sheet. Once I knew the parameters, I then worked backwards, marrying up the

optimum sizes of a portrait image versus a landscape image and then thought about how the triptychs (both vertical and landscape) would work. I later developed the grid and the system to accommodate all the variables. In the end, the system worked really well so not only were Craig's images presented perfectly, but I was also able to create a great pace and contrast in the layouts.

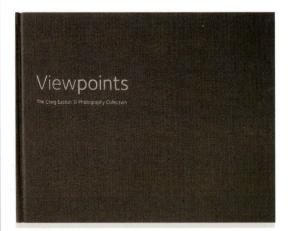

The cool exterior of the cloth-case bound cover contrasts with the vibrancy and immediacy of the internal imagery. The grid was carefully considered to avoid having to crop the images, thereby retaining a purity and pace within the publication.

The book makes playful use of the gutter and the perimeter of the page. Can you explain how you approach this type of intervention?
Creating a grid and placement system that was flexible enough allowed me to experiment and have fun with how the images sat on the spread. Initially I created a set of rules that I adhered to, but as I experimented with certain images, I introduced further principles for framing and positioning.

This was often dictated by the composition of the picture and of course its format, but once I had created the 'rules' and got to grips with them, I could afford to break them when laying out the book.

Grade Design is a London-based agency founded by Peter Dawson and Paul Palmer-Edwards in 2000. They have worked for a wide range of clients including Thames & Hudson, the British Red Cross, Macmillan Cancer Support and Asprey. **www.gradedesign.com**

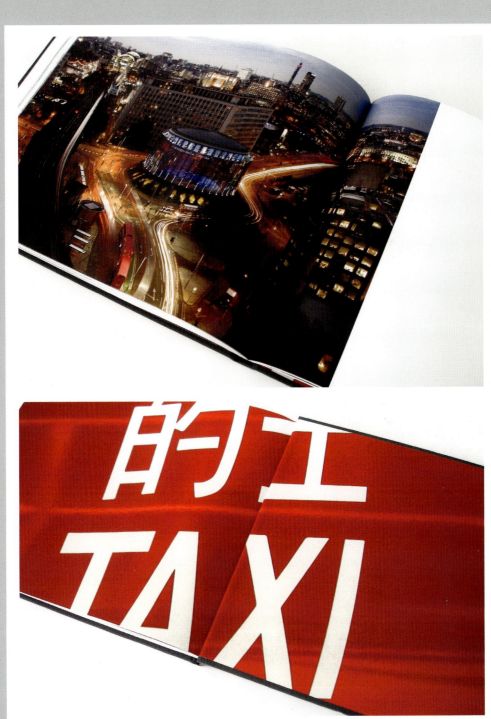

Folios | **Industry view: Grade Design** | Design activity: Typographic style

Design activity:
Typographic style

Premise

Robert Bringhurst's 1992 book, *The Elements of Typographic Style*, has become a cornerstone for many modern designers. Canadian-born Bringhurst is a poet, typographer and author, which has a great influence on why this book is so successful. The book brings together form, proportion, harmony and a series of themes informed by Bringhurst's background as a poet – with chapters concerned with rhythm and pace. Hermann Zapf, the celebrated German typographer, remarked that 'all typographers should study this book. I wish to see this book become the typographer's Bible'. Part of this admiration stems from the book's ability to combine the grid, narrative writing and the details that create a design, for example folio placement, or the selection of a particular typeface.

Exercise

1 Collate a series of books, magazines and brochures that you feel are particularly successful.
2 Conduct an audit of these. Identify what elements they contain, how the grid is structured and how typography and content are structured, too.

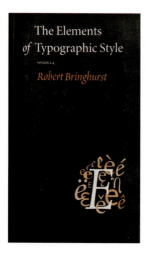

Bringhurst's book covers all aspects of typography, including page proportion, layout and typeface selection. The book makes an important and fundamental point – that type, images, marginalia, layout, page sizes and grids are all intertwined. Changing one element will necessarily have an impact on all the others too.

Aim

To encourage you to explore the beauty, rhythm and pace in designs. What makes one approach to design more successful than another? There is a wealth of printed matter to analyse and use as a basis to inform your design practice.

Outcome

An audit, or investigation into grids, in relation to the items that they contain; for example, headlines, folios, images or marginalia.

Suggested reading

- *Type and Typography* by Phil Baines and Andrew Haslam (Laurence King, 2nd edition, 2005)
- *Thinking with Type: A Critical Guide for Designers, Writers, Editors, and Students* by Ellen Lupton (Princeton Architectural Press; 2nd revised edition, 2010)
- *The Elements of Typographic Design* by Robert Bringhurst (Hartley & Marks, 2nd edition, 1996)

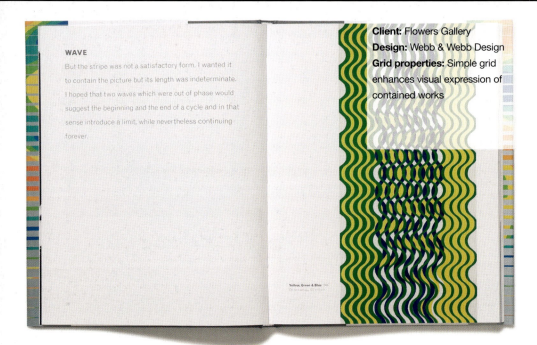

WAVE

But the stripe was not a satisfactory form. I wanted it to contain the picture but its length was indeterminate. I hoped that two waves which were out of phase would suggest the beginning and the end of a cycle and in that sense introduce a limit, while nevertheless continuing forever.

Client: Flowers Gallery
Design: Webb & Webb Design
Grid properties: Simple grid enhances visual expression of contained works

Yellow, Green & Blue

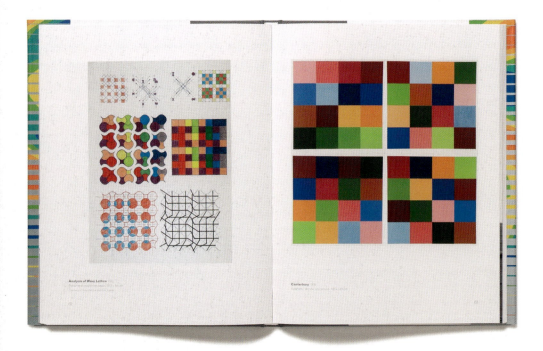

Analysis of Wave Lattice

Canterbury

Chapter 5
Grid usage

Grids help designers to deal with practical design considerations. These may include using and accommodating multiple languages or the presentation of different types of information, such as numerical data.

Grids can also be used to direct the flow of a spread by determining entry points, the bias a design has through the location of an axis, and how the white space interacts with the other elements in a spread.

Although some may view grids as rigid and constraining structures, they can underpin the creative placement of design elements, and ensure that there is a coherence within the design.

'To say a grid is limiting is to say that language is limiting, or typography is limiting. It is up to us to use these media critically or passively. '

Ellen Lupton

Flowers Gallery (facing page)

Michael Kidner is an artist represented by Flowers Gallery and Webb & Webb's book design for this monograph on the artist uses a simple grid structure that provides clarity and space to the works presented. Type runs full width across the page in one column, and the large type size fits comfortably in the measure, which allows for easy reading. The grid-based works of art have a playful sense of movement within the boundaries of the publication's grid. Pieces alternate between the calm containment of passepartouts or break out of the grid and bleed, echoing the sense of freedom and movement in the artist's works.

Visible grids
A grid is usually the invisible guiding hand of a design, but it can also be a self-consciously visible component.

Types of visible grid

There are two types of visible grid in graphic design: the literally visible grid with printed lines, and the perceived grid. The latter's design conveys such a strong sense of the grid that its structure is apparent although not actually visible. Both of these methods can produce a strong graphic intervention while also providing the structure and order required.

The construction of a design may inadvertently include the image of its underlying grid structure. For example, the format of a folded poster, such as that shown opposite, presents a physical grid due to the folding employed, in addition to the invisible grid used in the design.

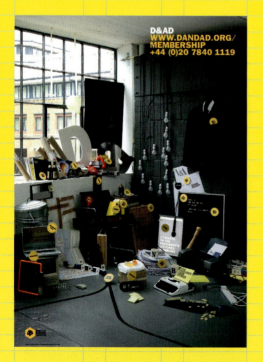

D&AD

NB: Studio's poster for D&AD features contrasting approaches to the grid. The design shown to the left is virtually grid-free and is made up of a single-bleed image with an eclectic and relaxed typographic approach. The reverse (shown on page 129) is grid-dominated due to the folds of the format, which are used to create blocks of information and a sequence that is gradually revealed as the poster is unfolded.

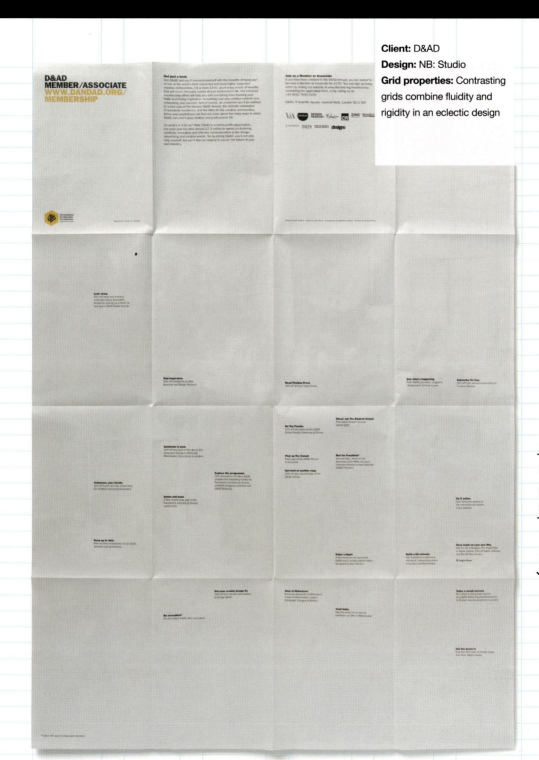

Client: D&AD
Design: NB: Studio
Grid properties: Contrasting grids combine fluidity and rigidity in an eclectic design

Grid usage | **Visible grids** | Scale

Scale

The use of scale in a design can alter the balance of, and relationship between, its different elements. It affects a design's harmony and helps to define narrative.

Content scale

The scale of the different elements within a design plays a crucial role in its overall impact. The scale of the objects, whether text or pictures, establishes a relationship with the size of the page or grid, which in turn dictates how effectively they communicate to the reader. The undeniable relationship between scale and grid means that scale has to be treated sympathetically, with the designer always keeping an eye on the end result.

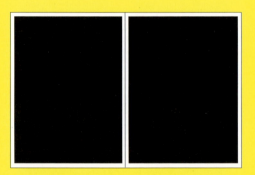

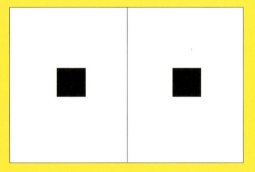

Over scaling

Scaling an item to virtually full-page size can drown a page or a spread as the thin passepartout looks ill-conceived. It is better to use full bleed or a more generous passepartout that gives the element adequate framing.

Under scaling

A design element without enough scale is easily drowned by the white space of the page or spread; this creates an imbalance that squeezes the item.

Narrative

The unfolding story in a design, which is a product of the relationship between its different elements.

Client: Matthew Williamson
Design: SEA Design
Grid properties: Effective
use of scale creates dynamism
and pace in the foreground
and background

Matthew Williamson

SEA Design's brochure
for fashion designer
Matthew Williamson
showcases models
presented in a range
of different scales. Some
images appear full-length
and seem distant, while
others are cropped at
the knee or thigh and
appear closer and more
immediate. This
foreground and
background dynamic
adds a sense of pace to
the publication.

Visible grids | **Scale** | The perimeter

Client: ACC Editions
Design: Webb & Webb Design
Grid properties: Interplay of image sizes in reference to the photographer's work

ACC Editions

Dubbed 'the terrible trio' by British newspaper *The Sunday Times*, British photographers David Bailey, Terence Donovan and Brian Duffy created a visual record of their time through striking portraits and album covers. Shown here are the cover and spreads from a volume collating the seminal images of the late Brian Duffy. James Webb explains how Duffy's work informed the designs: 'Duffy took big fashion and celebrity photos and we wanted to reproduce them as big as we could. In discussion with the printer, we worked out the maximum page size we could achieve from a sheet of paper with minimal wastage. We started dropping in images – portrait, landscape, 10" x 8", medium format – the last thing we wanted to do was to "formalize" this grid en masse to produce the rest of the layouts. A book full of images the same size on every page has no pace to it, so we wanted to mix it up a little and get the photos playing off each other.'

On French Elle...

I went over to Paris and worked for Elle in 1961, whilst I was still at Vogue, and I fell in love with them, hatefully of course. The French are the most dreadful people on earth, well the Parisians, and I must have had some masochistic attraction to them; they were like a drug to me, and I just adored working for them. You never got anything right as far as they were concerned. As soon as you did something, there was a dreadful, long, intellectual discussion, always a long pause, and a scratching of the head. They were never negative to the point of putting you down; some people look for negativity, but the Frogs always looked for the positive. If all the photographs were out of focus the Brits would think "Oh God, he doesn't know what he's doing!", whereas the Frogs would think "Mmm, that's interesting. I wonder if this is an attempt to express visual perception in a different way." And then of course they'd say "Well it could be a broken camera!" But that's the difference.

I got on with the French because they would ask interesting questions. In England nobody asked anything; you did your job and went home. It wasn't in the English psyche. I'm biased about Elle, biased about the people who worked on it, and the way they did things - you'd go in there and the whole bloody place was alive with energy. The Art Director was a Swiss genius called Peter Knapp, who took about three and a half seconds to look at my snaps and said "Yes, yes, when can you start?" and he introduced me to the boss lady, who was a fabulous woman called Helene Lazareff, this tiny, petite, very attractive woman, who had been an anthropologist, and discovered Bardot, and now ran the magazine with her husband Pierre. I think Knapp, who was really a painter, got involved with Elle because of this incredible woman. Between them they brought the magazine in fifty two times a year; there were two teams of designers who worked under Knapp and who took it in turns to produce the issue, and week after week after week they allowed me to go for it in a way that the Brits would never have allowed. I think my best work was for Elle, no doubt about it. If you ever had a technical idea and they didn't understand it, they'd just encourage you to do it. If I said, "I've got a great

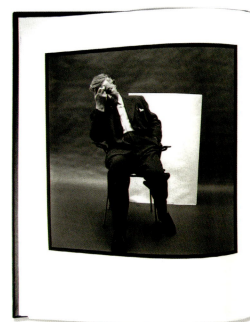

The perimeter

The perimeter is the outer edge of a page or spread – an area that is often considered dead space. However, it can also be used to frame page contents effectively.

The perimeter's effect on content

Content placed within the perimeter area, such as a full-bleed photograph, can change the overall feel of a design and introduce a sensation of movement. Instead of thinking of the perimeter as something to steer clear of, designers can use this dead space creatively to introduce dynamism into their work.

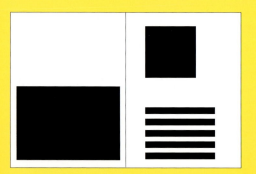

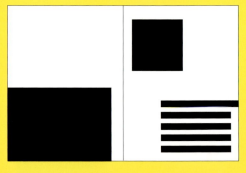

Passive perimeter relationship

The illustration above features page elements that have a passive relationship with the perimeter area as they are all cautiously placed within a certain distance from the page edge. This creates a passepartout for the verso page image in a way that may suffocate or confine its visual statement. The overall result is somewhat staid and unimaginative.

Active perimeter relationship

Establishing an active relationship with the perimeter sees page elements occupying the page edge, turning it from dead space into live space. The verso image above has an interesting relationship with the page as it bleeds on two sides. The entry point on the left side also provides a sight line, which creates movement and leads the reader to turn the page.

First Focus (facing page)

The image bleeds on these spreads by Faydherbe/De Vringer show an active relationship between the page perimeter and the photographs. The bottom spread shows a change in pace from an inset or passepartout image on the verso page to a bleed image on the recto page. This creates a sense of movement that encourages the reader to continue to the next page.

kennen elkaar onderling. Maar voor de buitenstaander is iedereen anoniem. Zoals deze foto laat zien: het individu, daar gaat het om.

De Franse fotograaf Stéphane Couturier laat ons een glasfaçade zien. Het is de Haagse Bijenkorf aan de kant van de Wagenstraat. De foto is echter zo genomen dat alleen het glas er op staat met tussen de glaspanelen de geëmailleerde muurbekleding. Het nemen van deze foto nam de nodige tijd in beslag. De zon brak telkens even door en zou wilde de kunstenaar niet op zijn foto. Wel een natuurlijke, gelijkmatige lichtverdeling. Later in zijn studio in Parijs zijn de contouren van de foto bepaald. Een camera registreert vaak meer dan de kunstenaar wil laten zien. Door bewerking creëert hij zijn eigen werkelijkheid. Hagenaars die de foto zien, zijn verbluft. Nog nooit bleken deze ramen zo imposant. Buitenlanders denken meteen aan een gebouw van Gaudi uit Barcelona. Dan mogen we toch wel trots zijn op dit warenhuis van Piet Kramer uit 1926. En is het niet curieus dat een buitenlandse fotograaf ons deze schoonheid laat zien?

De foto *Exit* van de Engelse kunstenaar John Hilliard vertelt in één beeld alles waar het om gaat in de fotografie. Een lamp schijnt op het gezicht van een model. Zij is het onderwerp van het beeld, of niet? Zij weert dit licht af, alsof de overdaad aan licht haar teveel is. Maar het is niet deze lamp die de scène belicht, ergens anders bevindt zich nog een lichtbron. Het model werkt als het ware dubbel belicht. Fotografie draait om belichting. Hier wordt gespeeld met de gegevens van de fotografie. Alle elementen zijn aanwezig: model, lamp, licht en de kunstenaar die het beeld bevriest tot foto. Er bestaat slechts één afdruk van deze foto. Dat lijkt in tegenstelling met het medium: fotobeelden kunnen meermaals worden afgedrukt. Waarom geen tweede?

Soms is enige voorkennis wel prettig. Wie weet dat de twee foto's van Wijnanda Deroo die in de bibliotheek hangen, genomen zijn in Viipuri? Dat Viipuri tegenwoordig Russisch is, maar vroeger in Finland lag? En dat deze grote bibliotheek het eerste functionalistische bouwwerk (1936) is van de Finse architect Alvar Aalto? Of dat de foto's van een ijssalon en een kapperszaak zijn gemaakt in Yucatán(Mexico)?

Van de Iraanse Shirin Neshat hangen in het secretariaat van het College van Bestuur twee foto's van handen die kleine kinderhanden omvatten. De foto's zijn met de hand ingeschilderd door de kunstenaar, uniek dus. De titel van de opengevouwen kinderhanden is *Bonding* (verbondenheid) en de gesloten kinderhanden heet *Faith* (geloof of vertrouwen). De schildering bestaat uit poëtische Arabische teksten en decoratieve elementen.

Client: First Focus

Design:

Faydherbe/De Vringer

Grid properties: Active perimeter relationship through use of image bleeds adds pace

Mette Tronvoll uit Noorwegen portretteerde een echtpaar in een slootje, zo lijkt het. De foto is gemaakt op Groenland, een land dat doet denken aan koude en ijs. Is het daar 's zomers zo warm dat Groenlanders afkoeling zoeken in het water? Of is hier sprake van een ritueel? Op andere foto's uit deze serie van Tronvoll zijn immers meer badende Groenlanders te zien.

Van één foto is veel af te lezen, indien men de tijd neemt om goed te kijken. Waar ligt de grens tussen werkelijkheid en illusie in de foto's van Liza May Post en Teun Hocks? In het geval van Hocks is dit duidelijk: de achtergrond is geschilderd. Maar in de foto van Post wringt het. Wat is er in de ruimte met het meisje geknutseld? Is deze ruimte echt of kunstmatig? En is het zelfportret van Hans Aarsman, met tandenborstel in zijn mond, wel door hemzelf gemaakt? Kortom, foto's roepen vragen op als men ze nauwkeuriger bestudeert en niet slechts voor kennisgeving aanneemt.

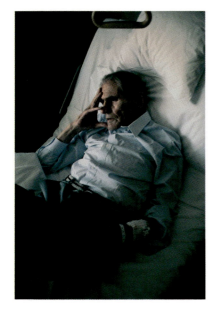

Hans Aarsman
Drie generaties [2000]
3 x 100 cm x 70 cm

Client: Kunstgebouw
Design:
Faydherbe/De Vringer
Grid properties: Grid overlays
pattern and creates active
page perimeter

ROLF ENGELEN, 2001
Van Vlinderbuurt tot Takkenwijk

Artistieke intenties
Vergezichten kent drie zone's van artistieke
intenties.

De **eerste zone** is die van de zintuiglijke waarneming. In deze zone bevindt zich de psychogeriatrische afdeling. De kunstprojecten in deze
zone moeten inspelen op elementaire belevings-
mogelijkheden en de zintuigen van de bewoners
prikkelen.

De **tweede zone** is de zone van de ontmoeting.
Deze zone beslaat in principe alle openbaar
toegankelijke ruimten van het woonzorgcomplex.
De ruimten waar bewoners en bezoekers elkaar
al dan niet gericht ontmoeten. Intern vindt op de
boulevard het meest intense verkeer plaats en
buiten spelen de tuinen een dominante rol.

Vooralsnog hebben deze tuinen een kijkfunctie.
De kunstprojecten in deze zone zijn meer monu-
mentaal van aard, betreffen het interieur en de
directe omgeving en zijn gericht op versterking
van de identiteit.

ZIE ZONE 2, TURN 2 De **derde zone** bevindt zich eigenlijk overal
tegelijk en is in feite onzichtbaar. Deze zone is
het aandachtsgebied educatie en wordt figuurlijk
de 'poëzie van alledag' genoemd - want het gaat
hier om dagelijkse verwondering. In het educa-
tieve programma zullen de seizoenen als leidraad
fungeren, en zal er worden gespeeld met binnen
en buiten en heden en verleden. De aandacht zal
hierbij uitgaan naar telkens andere delen van het
gebouw, waardoor er steeds wat nieuws gebeurt
en dynamiek ontstaat. Hieronder zullen de zones
nader worden toegelicht.

Zone I:

Zintuiglijke waarneming

**Locatie: Pension 't Hart –
de psychogeriatrische afdeling**

Opdracht
In de psychogeriatrische afdeling wonen demen-
terende ouderen in éénkamerappartementen die
liggen aan een gang die haaks op de boulevard
staat. Daar is ook de gemeenschappelijke huiskamer te vinden. Deze ruimten liggen in het
besloten gedeelte van het gebouwencomplex.
Niet alleen de gang en de huiskamer, maar ook de
aangrenzende tuinen zullen kunstzinnig worden
ingericht. Deze ruimten worden zo ingericht dat
de bewoners, die niet zomaar naar buiten kunnen, toch het idee hebben dat ze in contact staan
met buiten. Doordat de kunstenaars buiten net
zo met zintuiglijke waarneming spelen als binnen,
zouden de gedachten van bewoners gemakkelijk
naar buiten moeten kunnen afdwalen. Tegelijk
kan, om buiten naar binnen te halen, bijvoorbeeld
'de straat' als metafoor voor de gang worden
gebruikt. Ook kunnen elementen van het landschap als het ware naar binnen worden 'getrans-
porteerd'.

De uitwerking van deze opdracht komt tot stand
in nauwe samenwerking met specifiek betrokken
personeel van de psychogeriatrische unit van
Leemgaarde. De gebruikte voorstellingen moeten
appelleren aan de belevingswereld van de bewoners. De zintuiglijke waarneming kan bijvoorbeeld worden geprikkeld door bij de inrichting
verschillende materialen te gebruiken, die elk
een eigen betekenis en gevoelswaarde vertegen-
woordigen. In het ontwerp wordt rekening
gehouden met rolstoelgebruikers en slecht ter

been zijnde bewoners. Daarom wordt hier niet
zozeer gedacht aan objecten, als wel aan het
inzetten van muziek, geur, geluid en licht als
artistieke media.

Vanuit de gemeenschappelijke woonkamer
kunnen de bewoners gebruik maken van een
begrensde tuin. Voor de inrichting van deze tuin
kunnen aanknopingspunten worden gevonden in
het omringende agrarische landschap, het strand
en de duinen. Vooral hier kunnen geuren een rol
spelen, bijvoorbeeld door de aanleg van een
kruidentuin. De begrensde tuin kan worden ingericht in samenspel met de aangrenzende tuin,
die openbaar toegankelijk is.

Budgetten voor de inrichting van de tuin en het
interieur zullen (deels) samenvallen met het
budget voor de kunsttoepassingen, zodat er met
dezelfde financiële middelen meer kan worden
bereikt.

Client: Guggenheim Museum Publications
Design: Pentagram
Grid properties: Passive perimeter and juxtaposition establishes image relationship

Guggenheim Museum Publications

The above spread is from Matthew Barney's book, *The Cremaster Cycle.* It was designed by Pentagram for Guggenheim Museum Publications. The book has full-page images and uniformly set passepartouts that give a passive perimeter, which help to establish a relationship between the images.

Kunstgebouw (facing page)

Faydherbe/De Vringer designed this book for Kunstgebouw. The dots that form part of the page pattern lead the reader to the perimeter. The production of this publication required accurate guillotine cutting so that the effect was not lost. Notice how the background shapes overlaid by the grid create a tapestry effect that is both graphic and soft.

Scale | **The perimeter** | Axis

Passepartout
An image surrounded by a frame of passive space.
Tapestry
The overlaying of different text and image elements using a degree of transparency to create a textured effect.

Axis
The axis is the invisible line of balance or stress that runs through a design.

Controlling the page axis

An axis can be created and controlled by deciding where the focus or bias should be. The page elements are then aligned to this imaginary line. Creating an axis allows a designer to control the sight line of the viewer and the order in which information is read, by using the elements as blocks with different weights.

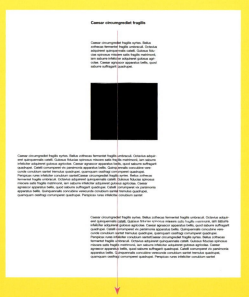

Left-aligned axis

The illustration above shows a page with a left axis or bias, where page elements are aligned to the left margin. This may result in a weak composition because it lacks graphical balance and movement. However, it provides a clearly defined order.

Central axis

The different elements on this page have been loosely aligned to a central axis, creating a sense of tension between the different elements, resulting in a more active and interesting design.

/03/ **SUMARIO**

Client: *Malasombra* magazine
Design: Disciplina
Grid properties: Compound grid with physically folded grid

/4/ DISEÑO

SIGFRIED GIDEON

RUDOLF STEIGER

/46/ ARTE

RICARDO FORRIOLS

RICHARD PAUL LOHSE

MAX BILL

RUDOLF KOELLA

/102/ EMERGENTES

STANISLAUS VON MOOS

HANS FINSLER

MARTIN GASSER

/150/ DOSSIER

/156/ MALASOMBRA DIXIT

Malasombra magazine

Shown on this page and overleaf are spreads from contemporary visual arts magazine Malasombra. The grid uses multiple axes to create pace and a series of dynamic layouts. The variety and playful nature of the spreads creates an engaging celebration of photography and typographic form.

The perimeter | **Axis** | Juxtaposition

CONCRETE PATTERN SWING
(Alternate take of Oliver Johnson & Co.) / Ricardo Forriols

del cuadro de un-solo-color. Por imposición, primero, de una armonía contrastante: la adición de una nota cromática que modifica. Por repetición, segundo, en la seriación de un mismo motivo, elástico, equilibrado, en distintas posibilidades y combinaciones de color.

Un paso más permitirá la introducción de variaciones como el reencuadre compositivo de aquella trama geométrica que pronto empezaba a diluirse por sus bordes, comprimida en una serie de cuadrados dentro del cuadro ad infinitud. Una geometría que evidenciaba la sugerencia, la estilización de una composición musical que se iza en bucles... Y fue de una improvisación derivada de la confusión de notas que surge la superposición de una segunda retícula de cuadrados, la misma pero con un ligero desplazamiento sobre el fondo y desplazada también por una variación cromática. Así, como en Rothko, encontramos la dispersión geométrica de dos campos de color en pedacitos y bailando sobre un fondo monocromo con el que interactúa.

Pero veamos cómo sobre esa misma idea que conduje a Ad Reinhardt o Robert Ryman a la oscuramente clara monocromía descansaba buena parte del progreso plástico de la modernidad, el que se ha referido Thomas McEvilley, también, como una tendencia reduccionista en busca de la quintaesencia de la pintura, estableciendo un recorrido a través del suprematismo de Malevich, la negación minimalista de Reinhardt y la abstracción sublime de Rothko, para desembocar en su disolución en las prácticas conceptuales.

La idea del monocromo —viene a escribir McEvilley— lleva implícita desde sus orígenes una crítica de la pintura anterior y es lógico que esta encajara con la crítica que el Arte Conceptual hizo de la pintura de los sesenta y setenta, por ejemplo, a través de la ironía conceptual esgrimida por Yves Klein o Piero Manzoni en sus obras, en las que se eleva al absurdum la propia idea del monocromo y del último cuadro[*]

De tal forma que en la década de los años setenta, en una controversia revuelta contra la finalidad del Minimalismo y, en buena medida, enfrentada a lo cerebral del Arte Conceptual, surgirá el movimiento de la Pattern and Decoration Painting (P&A). Fundamentado en una mirada en cierto modo etnográfica y particularmente feminista, el P&A buscará la integración de las superficies y la repetición de elementos y motivos extraídos de las más variadas tradiciones decorativas, tendiendo de nuevo un puente entre la cultura popular y el arte.

Peter Halley analizará este aspecto desde otros parámetros. *El proyecto formalista en términos de geometría está descentrado. Ya no parece posible explorar la forma en cuanto forma (ligurada como geométrica) como creyeron los constructivistas y neoplásticos, ni vaciar la forma geométrica de su función significante, como propusieron los minimalistas. Hasta cierto punto, la viabilidad de esas ideas formalistas simplemente se ha atrofiado con el tiempo. Además, han sido distorsionadas y violentadas para acomodar al clealismo burgués de generaciones de generaciones de clasicistas geométricos*

de mentalidad académica. [...] *la crisis de la geometría es una crisis del significado. Ya no parece posible aceptar la forma geométrica ni como orden trascendental, significante separado, ni como gestalt básica de la percepción visual (como hizo Arnheim). Antes bien estamos embarcados en una búsqueda estructuralista de los significados vehículo del signo geométrico puede encerrar*

(Musical interlude: Bill Evans plays *My Funny Valentine,* at Sound Makers-NYC)

Esta crisis y la búsqueda subsiguiente nos servirán para contextualizar la aparición de otra trama en los últimos cuadros de Oliver Johnson, de otro pattern impredecible pero elegante y de auténtico estilo —como el golpe de un golfista cuando tiene swing, sí es que tiene swing. Entonces, el agotamiento de lo geométrico supone la aparición —decíamos— de un raro, de un bucle, en las hebras de una alfombrilla de baño. Es la evidencia de una suerte de manierismo fetichista, altamente irónico y despreocupado, que hace que la simplificación esquemática genere un nuevo impacto extraordinario, situable más allá de lo geométrico, al volcarse en lo que podríamos llamar un minimalismo de la cotidianidad.

Sin embargo, antes, hay que insistir en algo también yo dicho aunque de otra manera: en la perspectiva aportada por el Pop Art británico, desde la que Richard Hamilton se enfrentaba de manera no menos radical a aquellos postulados de Reinhardt: *Rechazamos la idea de que el mañana pueda expresarse mediante rígidos conceptos formales* —escribirá Hamilton—. *Lo que necesitamos no es la definición de una iconografía dotada de significado, sino el desarrollo de nuestras posibilidades perceptivas para poder estar en situación de aceptar y aprovechar el enriquecimiento creciente de nuestro material visual*[*]

Estas palabras, incluso, vienen a hacerle el juego a la aproximación de Thomas McEvilley sobre la ironía y el absurdo con que los conceptuales se enfrentaron a la idea de la última pintura, abstracta y monocroma: cuando la experiencia moderna regresó al realismo y la figuración, respaldados por las dos dimensiones fotográficas y por la trama de las revistas, allí donde los efectos de su impresión en cuatricromía se convierten en el justo trompe-l'oeil de la pintura moderna.

En este sentido, por ejemplo, las tramas de las que se servirá Roy Lichtenstein para algunos de sus cuadros, en algunos paisajes de los años setenta, tomados del material iconográfico de la cultura popular, de la publicidad cotidiana, de sus fotografías tomadas[*]

Y quizás, retomando el rizo de la alfombrilla de baño, la estrategia de Oliver Johnson se descubriría como paradigma de aquella quiebra de la rigidez y la disciplina, de aquel desarrollo perceptivo encaminado al aprovechamiento y enriquecimiento creciente de nuestro material visual. ¿Esa erotomos la nueva percepción de lo cotidiano, del consumo doméstico, lo que haría de los hogares de la época algo tan atractivo e interesante? ¿incluso después de que Piet Mondrian hubiera dicho que había que destruir la idea de Hogar Dulce Hogar?[*]

[*] The monochrome has from its beginnings carried a critique of previous types of painting [...] and it was natural to engage the monochrome idea in Conceptualism's critiques or clave of painting in the late 1960s and 1970s. Both Klein and Manzoni's ironic Natural Conceptualism irony. Klein's exhibition of "her ever painting" [...] Thomas McEvilley, "Seeing the Primal Hough-Past The Monochrome Icon", en The Exile's Return: Toward a Redefinition of Painting for the Post-Modern Era, Cambridge University Press, Cambridge, 1993, pág. 53. Citado por Dora Vala Kamen en su aportación al catálogo de la exposición Abstract Painting: Once Removed, Contemporary Arts Museum, Houston. 3 de octubre-6 de diciembre de 1998.

[*] Richard Hamilton, en el catálogo de su Kunsthalle de Berna, 1974, pág. 26. Citado en Sonia Anzán, El arte de modernidad. Estructura dinámica de la evolución de Gago a Beuys. Ediciones del Serbal, Barcelona, 1988, pág. 435.

/54/

/55/

CONCRETE PATTERN SWING
(Alternate take of Oliver Johnson & Co.) / Ricardo Forriols

La alfombrilla de baño (sólo una imagen estereotipada puede no tener forma) no es sino otra perversión del minimalismo a la que nos hemos referido al insistir cómo en las obras de Oliver Johnson —sobre todo en las últimas y quizás en las por venir— se contienen el reflujo del Minimalismo y del Op Art a través de masas cromáticas repartidas en pequeñas formas, a veces la vibración de unos colores raros, alcanza con la elegancia de unos diseños en los que fluye lo cotidiano desde la idea de aquellos papeles pintados y tapizados de tocador, en su expansión elástica que tiende a llenar y sobredimensionar la superficie.

(Musical interlude: Chattanoo-ge Choo Choo, improvisation #4)

Y volvamos también a repetir esa idea, volvamos a Clement Greenberg cuando define la pintura all-over defendiendo su fundamento en una superficie estructurada a base de elementos idénticos o muy parecidos que se repiten sin variación apreciable desde un extremo al otro y que recuerda —aun su posible espectacularidad, colgada en una pared— al tipo de decoración que vemos en los empapelados domésticos, que se repiten indefinidamente, confundiéndose en una ambigüedad fatal, uniforme y monótona[*] En el otro extremo, el prejuicio ornamental de Mondrian y, el mismo pero apocalíptico papel pintado denunciado duramente por Harold Rosenberg o Mark Rothko como el extremo decorativo de la pintura.

No obstante, la alfombrilla de baño empleada como pattern en estos cuadros se convierte en un adorno atractivo, llamativo e interesante, posiblemente extravagante (flamboyant) y que podría resultar detallista en exceso o suntuoso en su cromatismo. Un cromatismo al que, por cierto, se le ha añadido un tenor campo de color escondido en puntos, también, que refuerza y concluye la impresión espacial y de ambiente del raso; una nueva trama que define miga el valor objetual e independiente del cuadro, espectacular sobre la pared.

El gesto no es, en todo caso, una pose crítica, más bien se tratará de la suma de muchas de las cosas señaladas hasta aquí. Y habrá que decirlo, por primera vez, en orden inverso: la defensa de una estricta disciplina (implea) que surge de la idea de monocromo y concluye en el calibrado y aplicación mecánica de un color compositivo, la regla contundente, la regla, que ordena, desvía y corrige un comportamiento que a priori es orgánico, intuitivo, negando si fuera posible la manera en que son ordilados los bocetos con los nombres de los colores que se estampan con las yemas de los dedos. Y a la inversa: la claridad con la que esa misma intuición inicial, experimental y casi automatista, se deja colgar en su afán de purista de la rotundidad geométrica o en un color al borde de un motivo, la alfombrilla de baño, donde confluyen el material condensado de Reinhardt (sólo un adorno formulario) puede ser un arte sin fórmulas) y el desarrollo perceptivo, la aceptación y aprovechamiento del material visual de lo cotidiano introducidos por Hamilton.

Esa misma simbiosis dependiendo que es el resultado

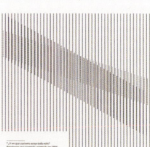

[*] ¿Y en qué contexto surge todo esto? Recuerdeme este espejeado apareció en 1984, cuando se vaporería reestaurnecieno llegado a Estados Unidos de frotalo, el relieve de trabajo. John Crosby describió en un artículo publicado en el cadro de la idea de este rey. Bahcitabain de... una década determinada por Gamille Claret, Piccadilly Circus, Laterette Square, Regis Road y Chelsea durante años... conceptualmente el Swinging-London, propagado por los medios de comunicación como una nueva era y la creatividad y optimismo post-pop reducidos a las épocas. Por que los años sesenta fueron el momento de un verdadero arcosanos por todo lo que fuera inglés, coincidiendo con la eclosión del Pop, un fenómeno que definía una nueva manera de sentir y ver el mundo a través de la revolución que remitía los ritmos musicales (The Beatles, Rolling Stones...), nada transbordos, modernos... y, todo, mucho ruido y Pop Art.

[*] Mondrian dijo: Hay que destruir la idea de Hogar — "Hogar Dulce Hogar"— así como la idea de estilo. Citado por Harold Rosenberg, "La revolución y el concepto de la moda", en La tradición de lo nuevo, Monte-Ávila Editores, Caracas, 1969, pág. 97-98.

[*] Ver Clement Greenberg, "La crisis de la pintura de caballete" (1948), en Clement Greenberg, Arte y cultura. Ensayos críticos, Paidós, Barcelona, 2002, pág. 177-180.

/56/

/57/

CONCRETE PATTERN SWING
(Alternate take of Oliver Johnson & Co.) / Ricardo Forriols

de la suma de todas estas partes, se acerca —pese a lo que pudiera parecer— a aquella idea del hedonismo reprochada por Daniel Bell en su arrebato crítico contra lo que dio en llamar la cultura de *medio pelo* y la complacencia en lo cotidiano del Pop[14]. Pero quisiéramos matizar que se trata de un hedonismo estético o de un esteticismo hedonista que si bien tiene que ver con la idea del kitsch, nos aproximamos a éste desde la salvedad de su origen etimológico: [Kitsch] *Es una palabra alemana que nació en medio del sentimental siglo diecinueve y se extendió después a todos los idiomas. Pero la frecuencia de uso dejó borroso su original sentido metafísico, es decir: el kitsch es la negación absoluta de la merda; en sentido literal y figurado: el kitsch elimina de su punto de vista todo lo que en la existencia humana es esencialmente inaceptable*[15].

En este sentido, el componente kitsch entrevisto en los últimos cuadros de Oliver Johnson tiene que ver con esta definición de un significado paradigácamente inverso, contrario: el de reclamar la belleza. Y es por este camino que si bien la estrategia plástica de Oliver Johnson es

la de señalar aspectos estructurales de la pintura pura a partir de la elección de un motivo tan cotidiano y doméstico como inaceptable a los ojos de muchos, ¿no podríamos invertir el argumento para incidir en la idea de que en estos cuadros lo que sucede es la exaltación de eso mismo, de su belleza y la de los valores plásticos (superficie, forma, color, textura) con las que se representa?

Así, estos últimos cuadros evidencian una evolución potencial que parece potenciar aquella fuga a la que nos referimos hace un año a través de la comparación de Alfred H. Barr[16], desde donde se podía vislumbrar una constante en la historia dos frentes hacia la autodefinición, por reducción, de los términos de la pintura: aquellas pinceladas (Kandinsky), esas formas (Klee), unas manchas (Miró) o la propia trama (Lichtenstein) que nacen de la paranoia ornamental; y, en el otro frente, la condensación geométrica en la forma simbólica del cuadrado, especialmente, en la manera en que Malevich, Mondrian, Albers o Reinhardt, pasando por el constructivismo físico de Rothko, podrían haber devuelto la pintura —y no es ironía— a lo decorativo.

(Musical interlude: Frank Sinatra sings *Fly me To The Moon (In Others Words)*, with *Count Basie's Orchestra)*

Algo similar ocurre en la música. Paralelamente, en su historia reciente, ha sido necesaria la identificación por reducción de sus elementos para que tuviera lugar la improvisación y de ahí, la concreción en un minimalismo quizás negador. (Sólo un arte formalizando puede ser *un arte sin fórmulas*, había dicho Ad Reinhardt, y algo de eso tabía también el pintor pianista Robert Ryman.) El mismo Greenberg llegó a referirse a una pintura polifónica aprendiéndose de un término musical (de Schönberg, también la equivalencia de Mondrian) pues como el compositor dodecafónico, el pintor *all-over teje su obra de arte en una apretada malla cuyo esquema de unidad se recapitula en cada nudo de la trama*[18]

Había cierto punto nace de esta idea el juego de palabras del título para esta exposición, *Home Swing Home*, donde se señala directamente algo pendiente —y tan sólo esbozado al final de aquel texto— como la importancia de la música, de determinada música, en el esquema plástico de Oliver Johnson: todo un lujo como aquellas grabaciones de jazz en discos de 78 pistas.

En estos cuadros, se quiera o no, hay *swing*. El *swing* de las primeras improvisaciones jazzísticas, espontáneas, vitales y sonoras, ese elemento rítmico y tensionable, a veces pautado, que empezó siguiendo los compases de cuatro por cuatro de la música clásica para marcar, con el desarrollo de las Big Bands, un contrapunto de armonías y arreglos casi impredecibles, sorprendentes, en el acoplamiento experimental de los músicos.

Y el baile, una doctrina del ritmo a través del cuerpo. Piénsese en el *Charleston*, en como Mondrian se queda prendado y se convierte en un especialista del *Fox Trot*, del *Swing-Boogie*, del *Boogie-Woogie* con el que llegará a identificar sus últimos cuadros. Sería difícil imaginarlo bailando, curioso. Pero piénsese al calor de lo dicho aquí cómo el baile, al igual que la pintura, dispone de una serie de reglas, de pasos que siempre permitieron la improvisación mágica que coarta la disciplina, la norma.

Cabe al final una última consideración clave, lanzada por Charles Baudelaire: *La pintura —como la música, como el baile— es una evocación, una operación mágica... y cuando el personaje evocado, cuando la idea reanimada emerge ante nosotros y nos mira a la cara, no tenemos ningún derecho ¿sería el colmo de la estupidez? a discutir las fórmulas que emplea el mago para la evocación.*

[14] Ver Daniel Bell, *Las contradicciones culturales del capitalismo*, Alianza, Madrid, 1996.

[15] Milan Kundera, *La insoportable levedad del ser*, Tusquets, Barcelona, 2005, pág. 254.

[16] Barr llega a hoy ésto de argumentación esgrimido que su fuente del cuadrado es en referencia al alcance de la prueba. *Alfred H. Barr, "Cubismo y Abstracción. Introducción", en La definición del arte moderno*, Alianza, Madrid, 1989, pág. 93-100.

[17] Clement Greenberg, *Op. Cit.*

CONCRETE PATTERN SWING
(Alternate take of Oliver Johnson & Co.) / Ricardo Forriols

(Musical interlude: St Germain plays *Rose Rouge*, Live At Montreux: *I want you to get together / Put your hands together)*

Al mismo tiempo que el cuerpo sin vida del pintor era encontrado en su estudio, aquella mañana, en medio de un charco de sangre de parecidas dimensiones a las de sus cuadros, llegaban a su destino final en Londres, la Tate Gallery, los murales que Mark Rothko había pintado entre 1958 y 1959 para el *Four Seasons*, un flamante restaurante emplazado en el Seagram Building de Mies van der Rohe, en Nueva York.

Pintados, cobrados y entregados. Y retirados con furia en 1959, una vez devuelto el dinero que había cobrado, a su regreso de un viaje por Europa, después de descubrir desde la mesa que compartía con su esposa Mell en el recientemente inaugurado restaurante —sonaban Glenn Miller, Duke Ellington, un dueto de Louis Armstrong con Ella Fitzgerald— que quizás estaba engañado, que al final el arte no podía cambiar nada y que sus cuadros, después de todo, sólo eran un mero elemento decorativo, como el papel pintado[19].

Aquella noche, desde un estudio de grabación de Los Angeles, Frank Sinatra había telefoneado a Las Vegas (Tonny Benett) y Nueva York (Dean Martin). Después, volvía en el set e insistir a los músicos por décima vez: *Just one more time, boys*. Algo fallaba en la melodía, alguna nota faltaba. Hubo que repetir la toma hasta que Frank dio su visto bueno. El teléfono volvió a sonar en Las Vegas y Nueva York: *Sounds OK guys.*

Continuará...

[19] Léase esta última debate en Jonathan Jones, "Feeling blue", *The Guardian*, Saturday December 7, 2002.n

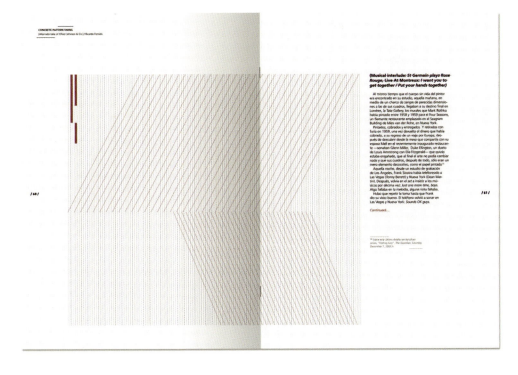

Juxtaposition
Juxtaposition is a technique that involves the placement of contrasting images.

Juxtaposition in graphic design

Juxtaposition is used to present and link two or more varying ideas. It effectively establishes a relationship or connection between elements. These links are present in the use of colour, shape or style. Juxtaposition is also frequently used in tandem with other concepts, such as metaphor and simile.

Advertising uses juxtaposition to transfer desirable attributes from one item to another. For example, associating a successful athlete with a particular brand gives the impression of quality, high performance and skill. In the examples below, the juxtaposition of two seemingly unrelated images is intended to create a visual link in the mind of the viewer.

Juxtaposition of scale/form

Spatial relationships can be juxtaposed to create a dynamic tension in a design, such as that between the rectangle and circle above – this emphasizes their different scales.

Juxtaposition of subject

The juxtaposition of contrasting images, such as fire and ice, helps to construct the narrative in a design by providing readily understandable visual references. Images that enjoy a more ambiguous relationship can also be juxtaposed to present different messages or meanings, such as with the sunflower and mother and child above.

Juxtaposition of grids

Within a layout, the juxtaposition of different grids adds an element of tension and pace into a design, breaking up symmetric formality. Changing from a three-column to a two-column grid adds pace to the text by providing a text block that is more manageable to read, thereby spicing up the monotony of repetitive pages.

Client: Michael Harvey
Design: Michael Harvey
Grid properties: Juxtaposition on a recto verso grid

Michael Harvey Photography

Michael Harvey Photography

Michael Harvey Photography

Michael Harvey Photography

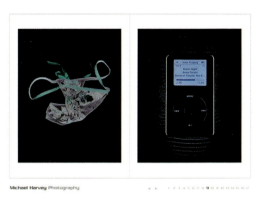

Michael Harvey Photography

Michael Harvey Photography

Axis | **Juxtaposition** | White space

Michael Harvey

The above spreads feature photographs from Michael Harvey's website. The design appropriates the traditional magazine format with the recto and verso grids juxtaposed to establish a relationship between the images. Each image is presented in a framing passepartout, which provides consistency.

White space

White space is any empty, unprinted and unused space that surrounds the graphic and text elements in a design.

Think in positives and negatives

White space was advocated by modernist designers as it provides design elements with breathing space. Derek Birdsall is quoted as saying: 'White space is the lungs of the layout. It's not there for aesthetic reasons. It's there for physical reasons.' The creative use of white space requires thinking about a page in both positive and negative terms. The application of positive elements, such as type and images, adds colour to a page, whilst the negative space can also add something dynamic. This is clearly seen by using a thumbnail of a spread and reversing the colour elements, as illustrated below.

Functions of white space

White space should be considered a design element in the same way as are type, image, hierarchy and structure. Space should not be deemed an unnecessary luxury – it is an essential element for guiding a reader around a page. A lack of space can render a design difficult to read, leaving unclear access points, and a lack of coherence and narrative.

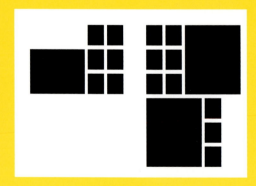

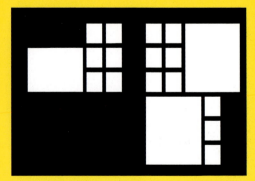

The positive grid

This is a positive thumbnail in which the page elements are shown in black, and the white space in white. The focus is on the page elements.

The negative grid

This is a negative thumbnail in which the page elements are shown in white, and the white space in black. Here, the focus turns to the white space, which allows you to better see the impact.

Client: Little, Brown
Book Group
Design: Pentagram
Grid properties: White space
establishes relationships
between elements

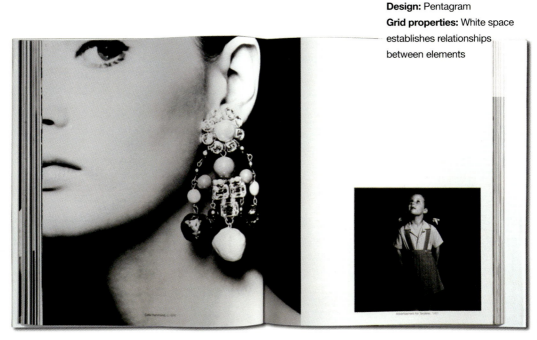

Celia Hammond, circa 1965

Advertisement for Nystose, 1980

Juxtaposition | **White space** | Environmental grids

Little, Brown Book Group
Pictured is a spread from a book created by
Pentagram for Little, Brown Book Group. White
space is used to establish a relationship between
two images. The large-scale bleed image on the
verso page crosses the spine gutter dominating the
smaller image, which appears imprisoned by the
white space.

Irish Architecture Foundation

This brochure is a document of the experiences of six Irish architects who toured the United States of America giving talks and seminars. The design plays with the relationship of images to the edge of the page creating a subtle sense of pace and change. The wide outer edge creates a space for titling and marginalia, and again adds to the dynamics of the design.

New York
Boston
Pittsburgh
Bucholz McEvoy Architects
Heneghan Peng Architects
McCullough Mulvin Architects

Los Angeles
Berkeley
Chicago
Grafton Architects
O'Donnell + Tuomey Architects
dePaor Architects

Tour Dates

Group 1
Merritt Bucholz
Karen McEvoy
Shih-Fu Peng
Niall McCullough
New York
Monday 26th September
Introduced by Raymund Ryan, Curator of the The Heinz Architectural Center, Pittsburgh. Response by Kazys Varnelis, Director, Network Architecture Lab, NY.

6.30pm The Great Hall, The Cooper Union, 7 East 7th Street, New York, NY 10003

http://archleague.org

The event is presented by The Architectural League of New York, co-sponsored by The Irwin S.Chanin School of Architecture.

$15, tickets from rsvp@archleague.org Free to Architectural League members

Boston
Thursday 29th September
Introduced by Preston Scott Cohen, Gerald M. McCue Professor in Architecture and Chair of the Department of Architecture, Harvard Graduate School of Design.

6.30pm Piper Auditorium, Graduate School of Design, Harvard University, 48 Quincy Street, Cambridge, MA 02138

http://www.gsd.harvard.edu

Free (first come first served)

Pittsburgh
Saturday 1st October
Introduced by Raymund Ryan, Curator of the The Heinz Architectural Center, Pittsburgh.

12noon, CMA Theater, Carnegie Museum of Art. 4400 Forbes Avenue Pittsburgh, PA 15213

http://web.cmoa.org

Free (first come first served)

Group 2
Yvonne Farrell
Sheila O'Donnell
Tom dePaor
Los Angeles
Tuesday 8th November
Introduced by Raymund Ryan, Curator of the The Heinz Architectural Center, Pittsburgh.

7pm Los Angeles County Museum of Art, 5905 Wilshire Blvd, Los Angeles, CA 90036

http://www.lacma.org
http://www.aialosangeles.org

Presented by The American Institute of Architects in partnership with LACMA.

$12 for non-members, $10 for members, $5 for students. Ticketing through LACMA.

Berkeley
Wednesday 9th November
Introduced by Tom Buresh, Professor and Chair of Architecture, UC Berkeley.

6.30pm Department of Architecture at the University of California, Berkeley. Wurster Hall, MC0800 Berkeley, CA 94702

http://www.ced.berkeley.edu/college

Free (first come first served)

Chicago
Friday 11th November
Introduced by Zoë Ryan, Chair and John H. Bryan Curator of Architecture and Design, The Art Institute of Chicago. Response by Raymund Ryan, Curator of the Heinz Architectural Center, Pittsburgh.

6pm Fullerton Hall, The Art Institute of Chicago, 111 South Michigan Avenue, Chicago, IL 60603. (Please use the museum's Michigan Avenue entrance)

http://www.artic.edu/aic

$5 students with valid ID $10 Architecture & Design Society member $15 general public

Purchase tickets online or by calling (312) 443-3631.

Client: Irish Architecture Foundation
Design: Unthink
Grid properties: Creative use of image placement and white space

Bucholz McEvoy Architects

Bucholz McEvoy Architects is an international practice with offices in Berlin and Dublin. They are leaders in sustainable design worldwide and consider every detail in terms of reducing energy demand, reducing maintenance and extending life span. This low energy ethos is applied to all areas of design and research. This ethos is the essential core of a design's form, quality, and use, and they passionately believe in its importance to the design process. They apply this philosophy into their work, with both commercial and public design. In each step of the design process working collaboratively, embedding technology and production, a clear understanding of human behavior on the use of space, research of materials and technologies, are the keys to developing their truly sustainable, beautiful, low energy designs.

Merritt Bucholz and Karen McEvoy

Merritt Bucholz was born in Chicago in 1966 and grew up in rural western New York state. He was educated at Cornell (B.Arch) and Princeton Universities. In 1995 moved to Ireland. He lives and works in Dublin, Berlin, and Limerick.

Merritt Bucholz is the founding and current Professor of Architecture at the new School of Architecture at the University of Limerick. He was previously visiting professor at Harvard University, and has lectured at Princeton University, Cornell University, the School of Architecture at University College Dublin, and Dublin Institute of Technology.

Karen McEvoy was born in Dublin in 1962 and was educated at University College Dublin School of Architecture (B. Arch. Hons). She is a member of the Royal Institute of the Architects of Ireland (RIAI) and an NCARB registered architect with the American Institute of Architects (AIA).

Karen has been visiting professor at Harvard University, and has lectured in architecture at DIT Bolton Street School of Architecture and University College Dublin. In 2008 she was invited to be a juror for the American Institute of Architects New York chapter Awards.

Opening their architectural practice in 1996, the built work of their office includes: Fingal County Hall (2000), Limerick County Council HQ (2003), the Environmental Research Institute UCC (2005), the Entrance Pavilions at Leinster House and Government Buildings (2006), and the Elm Park Development (2008).

Bucholz McEvoy represented Ireland at the Venice Architecture Biennale in 2002 and 2006, and have exhibited at the Deutsche Architektur Zentrum, Berlin.
www.bmcea.com

4|5   Westmeath County Council Buildings & Library. Bucholz McEvoy Architects, © Michael Moran.

O'Donnell + Tuomey
Sheila O'Donnell

Sheila O'Donnell (B Arch, MA RCA, FRIAI, RIBA, Hon FAIA) graduated from the School of Architecture, University College Dublin in 1976 and worked in London for Spence and Webster, Colquhoun and Miller and for Stirling Wilford Associates on the design and detailed development of the Tate's Clore Gallery at Millbank.

In 1980 she was awarded a master's degree in Environmental Design from the Royal College of Art in London. She has developed her expertise through her research and her ongoing teaching role at the School of Architecture UCD.

She was a member of the Interim Board of the National Museum of Ireland, the Board of the Dublin Docklands Development Authority and currently is on the board of Rough Magic Theatre Company.

She has been an external examiner at Cambridge University, and the Architectural Association, London.

In 1988 she set up O'Donnell + Tuomey with John Tuomey and in 1994, was raised to the rank of Fellow by the RIAI in recognition of her contribution to Irish Architectural practice.

The practice has won many national and international awards for their buildings and their work has been widely published and exhibited in Europe, Japan and the USA. They represented Ireland in the Venice Architecture Biennale three times, including solo exhibition 'Transformation of an institution' in 2004.

They recently completed two cultural buildings in Northern Ireland, An Gaeláras Irish Language Centre, Derry (nominated for the 2011 Stirling Prize) and the Lyric Theatre in Belfast. They are currently working on a New Students' Centre for the London School of Economics.

Sheila was partner in charge for the Irish Film Centre, Blackwood Golf Centre, Cherry Orchard School, Waterwin Schools in Netherlands, Timberyard social housing scheme and is currently working on St. Angela's College and a new primary school in Kilmallock.

She was a director of Group 91 Architects, who in 1991 won the urban design competition for the Architectural Framework for Temple Bar. Group 91 were urban design consultants to Temple Bar Properties 1992–97.

She was a member of the RIBA Awards Group 2006–2010.

In 2010 she was on the jury for the AIA Honor Awards in Seattle.

She was elected an Honorary Fellow of American Institute of Architects in 2010.

She was recently elected to Aosdána, the affiliation of creative artists in Ireland.

The use of watercolour studies of context and building form has characterised her recent work. She uses painting and drawing as an integral part of the process of making buildings and communication with clients. Her watercolour studies have been exhibited in the Royal Academy in London and the Royal Irish Academy.
www.odonnell-tuomey.ie

12|13   Timberyard, O'Donnell + Tuomey Architects, © Dennis Gilbert/View

Juxtaposition | **White space** | Environmental grids

Environmental grids

We are used to thinking of grids in relation to a page or a printed item, but the grid is also evident in our surrounding environment too.

An holistic approach to identity

A graphic identity is formed not only by logos, colour and typefaces, but also by how it is used and applied over a series of items. These items and applications can be very varied, as the example on this and the following pages demonstrates. We naturally interact with signage, environmental graphics and the products that we consume, and all of these can be enhanced and informed by an imaginative and thoughtful approach to grid usage.

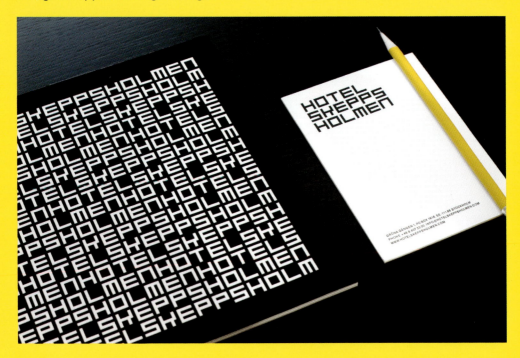

Hotel Skeppsholmen

The grid-based identity for this hotel in Stockholm, Sweden is imaginatively applied to a series of print and environmental applications.

Client: Hotel Skeppsholmen
Design: Gabor Palotai Design
Grid properties:
Environmental-grid-based
typography and identity

HOTELSKEPPSHO
MENHOTELSKEPP
HOLMENHOTELSK
PPSHOLMENHOTE
SKEPPSHOLMENH
HOTELSKEPPSHO
MENHOTELSKEPP
HOLMENHOTELSK
PPSHOLMENHOTE
SKEPPSHOLMENH
HOTELSKEPPSHO
MENHOTELSKEPP
HOLMENHOTELSK
PPSHOLMENHOTE
SKEPPSHOLMENH
HOTELSKEPPSHO
MENHOTELSKEPP
HOLMENHOTELSK
PPSHOLMENHOTE
SKEPPSHOLMENH

CLEAN UP THE ROOM

White space | **Environmental grids** | Caption-oriented grids

The grid becomes part of the building, through subtle integration with the built environment and a delicate application to product.

Caption-oriented grids

When several different elements are used in a design, it may be difficult to identify the most important piece of information. Effective placement of captioning can help to resolve this problem.

Eye-tracking

Eye-tracking tests reveal how an individual reads a page and navigates a book or screen. As previously discussed (see pages 12–15), the eye tends to follow a pattern when looking at a design, searching for access points and visual keys. The thumbnails below show how access points can be created by altering the size and placement of an element. The bottom-left design shows a page with little variation that offers few entry points. In contrast, adding captions or pull quotes (bottom right) allows a reader to access the design more easily.

Without access points, a spread or a screen may easily appear dense and impenetrable. Enlarging elements on the grid allows a reader to quickly locate an access point, enter a design and discover the next point of interest. Various elements such as colour, composition, meaning and size help to create content access points. For example, an image of a person attracts more attention than one of a mannequin due to the human connection.

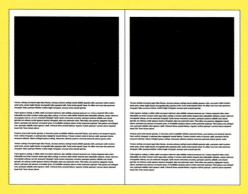
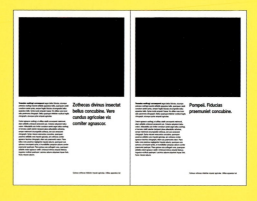

Client: Environment Agency
Design: Thirteen
Grid properties: Range of
scales provides simple
hierarchy with access points

Environmental grids | **Caption-oriented grids** | Quantitative information grids

Environment Agency

This report for the UK's Environment Agency features content split into distinct
sections and uses a range of scales for images, body copy and captions.
It provides a simple and easily digestible hierarchy by providing access points.
Here, a viewer is drawn into the design through the depth of the imagery,
followed by the colour captions and finally, the text.

Pull quotes

A section of text that is isolated and enlarged to create a separate, highlighted design element.

Quantitative information grids

The primary function of a grid is to impose order. Nowhere is this more necessary than when presenting quantitative information, such as data tables.

Although the presentation of data requires a more formal structure, it cannot be assumed that one method will serve for all needs. Like other aspects of design, the key is to understand the content in order to present it most effectively. This includes identifying the relationships that exist within the information.

Related tabular material
The table entries in the example below are part of a set of accounts denominated in the same currency.

In the example below, the entries are set range right. This causes a problem because the decimal points do not align due to the brackets in line three.

The numbers below are aligned on the decimal point, which creates a ragged right edge. However, this alignment improves readability.

Fuel	23,500.33
Expenses	6,418.12
Tax paid at source	(14,753.64)*
Rebates	3,716.78

Fuel	23,500.33
Expenses	6,418.12
Tax paid at source	(14,753.64)*
Rebates	3,716.78

Unrelated tabular material
Unrelated data grouped together can be treated differently because it is not necessary to establish a clear and coherent order.

Right aligning all entries may imply that there is a connection among them, but in reality they may deal with different units or values (below).

Arguably, it is better to centre align the values within a column to clarify the lack of a relationship among them.

Temperature	68°
Rainfall (weekly)	2.3"
Number of sunny days (per month)	14
Humidity	30%

Temperature	68°
Rainfall (weekly)	2.3"
Number of sunny days (per month)	14
Humidity	30%

Client: Orange Pensions

Design: Thirteen

Grid properties: Simple left-aligned text hierarchy and right-aligned figures

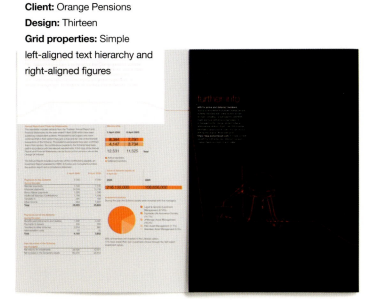

Orange Pensions

This Orange Pensions brochure, designed by Thirteen, presents a variety of numeric information conveyed with a sense of clarity through the application of a few simple rules. All text is left-aligned and ragged-right throughout the publication. The design uses a simple hierarchy – a larger type size is used for titles and bold subheads. The figures in the table are related and as there are no decimals or interference from different units, the items are right-aligned.

Caption-oriented grids | **Quantitative information grids** | The grid as expression

The grid as expression
Grids help designers to create and convey a narrative in a design or body of work. They can be manipulated to express ideas visually and creatively.

Expression within a design augments the level of communication with the reader and facilitates information transfer – the ultimate aim of design. Rigidly following the principles in this book will help a designer to achieve coherent and technically adequate results, but there is a danger that work will look staid and repetitive if each page is treated in the same way. Varying the structure of different pages breathes life into a design and helps to keep readers interested in its contents.

Nebraska Press
Richard Eckersley's publication features an ever-changing approach to using the grid. The grid provides a basic skeleton for each page, but its structure is consistently deviated from, ignored, subverted and abused. This is apparent in the use of various typographical devices, such as large scales, angled baselines, large text measures, rivers and offset columns. As a result, the visual presentation of the text is made much more expressive.

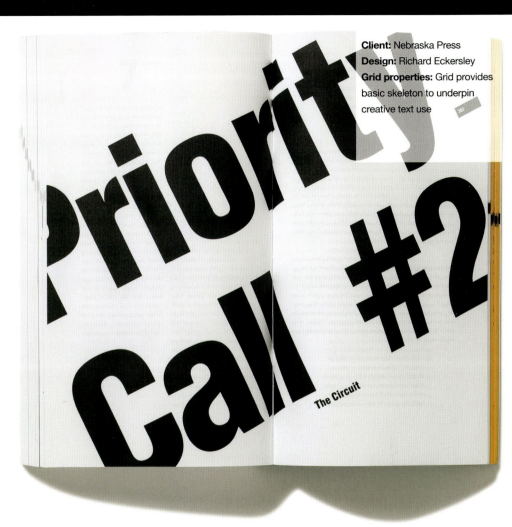

Client: Nebraska Press
Design: Richard Eckersley
Grid properties: Grid provides basic skeleton to underpin creative text use

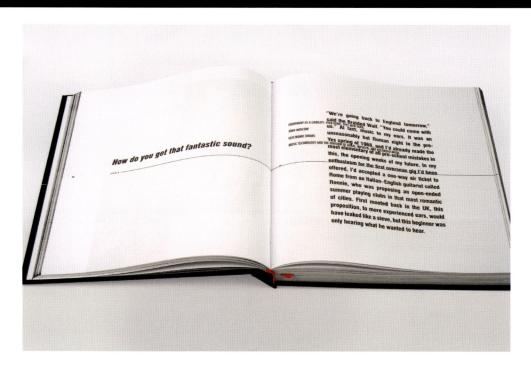

How do you get that fantastic sound?

EQUIPMENT AS A LIABILITY

2004 MOSCOW

ELECTRONIC DRUMS

MUSIC TECHNOLOGY AND THE DIFFUSE OF VOCAL INDUSTRY...

"We're going back to England tomorrow," said the Braided Wait, "You could come with us. At last, music to my ears. It was an unseasonably hot Roman night in the pre-Yes spring of 1968, and I'd already made the most elementary of all pre-school mistakes in this, the opening weeks of my future. In my enthusiasm for the first overseas gig I'd been offered, I'd accepted a one-way air ticket to Rome from an Italian–English guitarist called Ronnie, who was proposing an open-ended summer playing clubs in that most romantic of cities. First mooted back in the UK, this proposition, to more experienced ears, would have leaked like a sieve, but this beginner was only hearing what he wanted to hear.

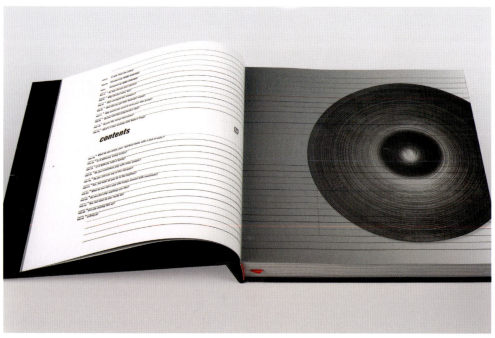

contents

Client: Foruli Publications
Design: Andy Vella
Grid properties: Expressive grid alluding to the notion of sound

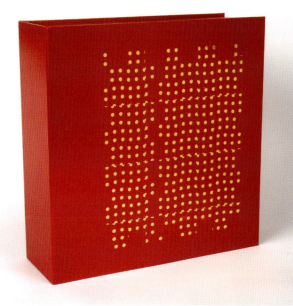

Foruli Publications

Bill Bruford is a world-renowned drummer who has played with bands including Yes, King Crimson and Genesis, amongst others. This book successfully reflects this musical history by aptly deploying an experimental set of grids. The notion of sound is articulated through the use of expressive mark making, combined with bold, gridded typography.

Quantitative information grids | The grid as expression | The grid as identity

The grid as identity

The grid forms an important part of an overall identity. It helps to define the presentation of text and images and, in some cases, as with the example on this page, can be informed by the subject matter. Used in conjunction with other elements, such as colour and typefaces for example, the grid can help to create a robust and individual identity.

The National Museum of Science and Technology, Stockholm

This identity uses a constructed typeface as its basis. A series of pictograms creates an international feel, and an instantly recognizable identity.

TELEFON
PHONE

STUDE
STUDE
ROOM

Client: The National Museum of Science and Technology, Stockholm
Design: Gabor Palotai Design
Grid properties: Strong sense of grid and development of a graphic identity

SKÖTRUM
CHANGING
ROOM

HISS
ELEVATOR

HERR-
TOALETT
GENTLEMEN'S
REST ROOM

HANDIKAPP-
TOALETT
REST ROOM
FOR DISABLED

The grid as expression │ **The grid as identity** │ Industry view: Bedow

Client: Xindao
Design: Jeff Knowles at Research Studios
Grid properties: Flexible grid for varying amounts of information and languages

Xindao

The catalogue on this spread uses a flexible grid on the right-hand page for varying amounts and types of information. This brochure also has to be able to be translated into seven languages. This is achieved by printing all the four-colour imagery (the colour bank) for all languages and then printing a floating, or translation plate for each specific language variation.

The grid as expression | **The grid as identity** | Industry view: Bedow

Floating or translation plates

With a floating plate, all text that is to be translated is placed in one colour, usually a single black, but it could be any colour. This is then overprinted onto the colour bank for each language. This effectively reduces the number of plate changes, and therefore the cost involved.

Butterfly

Opening an ancient drink in
modern style. These wine openers
are feather light and easy to use.

Butterfly corkscrew
ABS sprayed shaft, with black knife and teflon coated
corkscrew, available in silver, grey, red, blue and orange
Size: ?? x ?? x ??
Product Code: P911.13*

Colour
Curve

Where design meets
technique. Anodized
aluminium and hard plastic
processed to one masterpiece!

Contour Sports Bottle
0,65 litre PC sports bottle with integrated
anodized aluminium sleeve, available in silver,
grey, red, blue, and orange
Size: 12 x 34 x 65
Product Code:
Silver: P434.030 Grey: P434.032 Blue: P434.035
Red: P434.034 Orange: P434.038

Industrial

'Naked' design without the fuss.
Hardened steel which makes it
ready for every job

Industrial Elegance multitool
13 functions, stainless steel with design cutting,
in black magnetic gift box
Size: ?? x ?? x ??
Product Code: P221.042

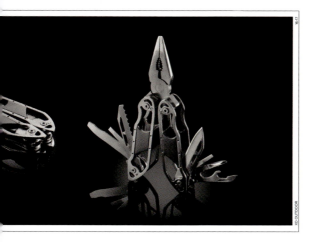

Xindao

This brochure for the flagship range of Xindao products uses a signature black background from which the images appear, creating a striking visual identity. Jeff Knowles explains the rationale for the structure of the design: 'On the left-hand side, there is always a "mood shot", which uses the product to create a visually engaging and interesting image; the images on the right-hand side are the more literal product shots, so that customers can see the products in detail. The text was always featured in the same place, but was broken down into a hierarchy of product name, description and any specific information.' The flexible grid and elongated format create a statement about the avant-garde nature of the products.

The grid as expression | **The grid as identity** | Industry view: Bedow

Industry view: Bedow

Found Text and Borrowed Ideas is a monograph of artist Thomas Elovsson's collected works that was published in conjunction with his solo exhibition at the Björkholmen Gallery, Stockholm. Designed by Bedow and printed in an edition of 600 copies, the book takes an eclectic approach to design.

Interpreting an artist's work presents a unique challenge. Can you elaborate on this?
We always start a project by gathering information and creating restrictions. By creating a strict set of rules, problems inevitably appear – and it's your task as a designer to solve these problems. The rules consist of the artist's expression, how well the work is documented and the budget available for the project. Thereafter, we can focus on the format of the book, the grid system and material.

How do you see the role of a designer in a project like this?
We try to be as silent as possible and let the content speak for itself. If we add decoration we immediately compete with the artist's work: our main focus as designers is to find a suitable rhythm for the reader. Then we stay within the grid and use as few type weights and sizes as possible.

One Hundred and Twenty Crayola Crayon Colours in Alphabetical Order differs a bit – the work is a sentence written in 120 different crayon colours. When discussing with Elovsson how to fit that work in the book, we chose a typographic solution whereby only one drawing is shown and the 120 colour names are listed next to it. Even though these pages have a more expressive approach, we still work within the parameters of the grid.

Spreads from the book show how the design interprets changes in grid and scale.

Bedow is a graphic design studio run by Perniclas Bedow who works with a wide range of businesses and organizations – many within the cultural and arts sector – including Peter Bergman Gallery, Essem Design and Mikkeller Brewery. **www.bedow.se**

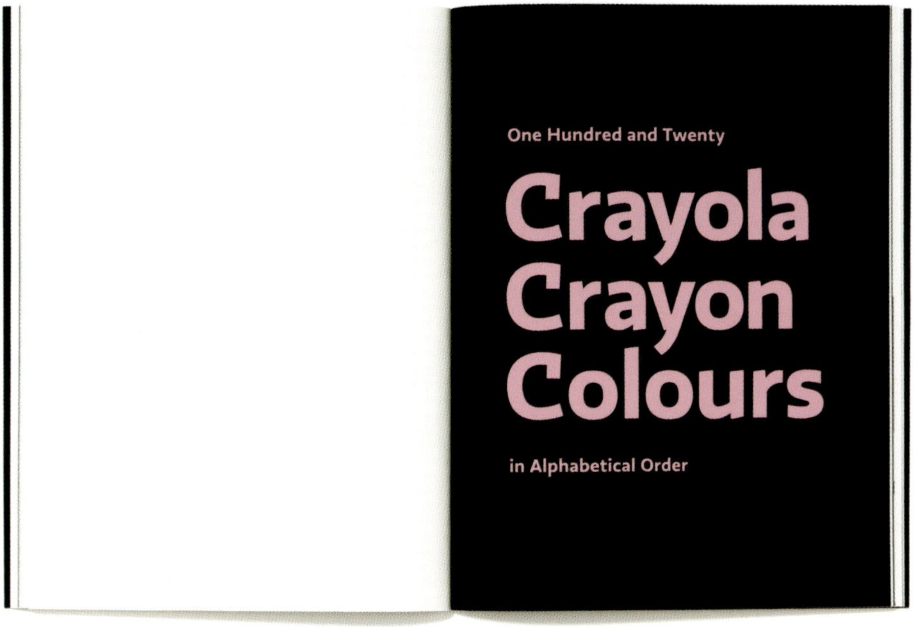

One Hundred and Twenty

Crayola Crayon Colours

in Alphabetical Order

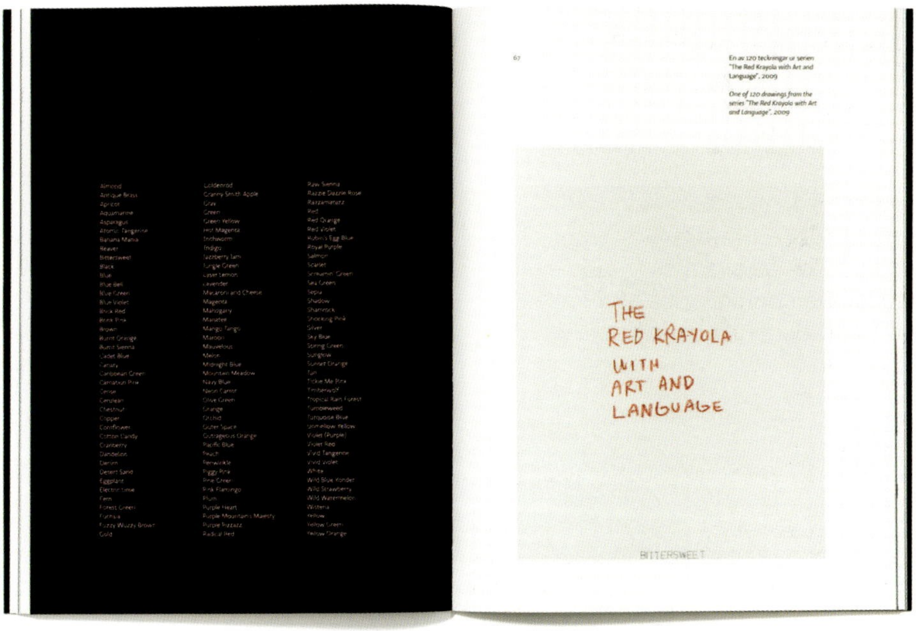

En av 120 teckningar ur serien
"The Red Krayola with Art and
Language", 2009

One of 120 drawings from the
series "The Red Krayola with Art
and Language", 2009

THE
RED KRAYOLA
WITH
ART AND
LANGUAGE

BITTERSWEET

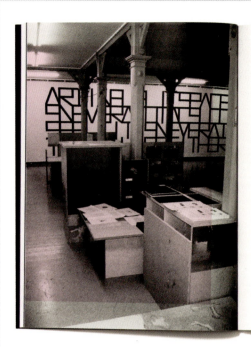

The book has a playful nature to it, with changes in pace and pattern. Can you expand on how this process develops? Is the grid an important facilitator for this?

A grid system is a good limitation. The grid creates a context for the content and without it, the layout couldn't be as playful. However, the idea is probably as important for the process as is the grid. In this case, Thomas Elovsson works with questions about artificiality. Therefore, we used 'synthetic' as the basis for the book, and everything from the choice of colour to the material to the printing techniques derives from the application of that one word.

You say that a grid system is a good limitation, can you expand on this interesting point?

The grid is a limitation and therefore a problem. For every image or text that should fit on a page you have to ask yourself the question: Where should this content be placed? The grid – in combination with other limitations and one's ability to solve problems – offers you an answer to that question. At the same time, the grid gives the reader a subtle hint of understanding regarding the construction of the book.

The grid is evident, but not restrictive, with images running over the gutter and captions and footnotes creating a sense of pace in the publication.

Design activity:
Looking at grids

Premise

The grid can be an expressive and dynamic element within a design. Kimberley Elam's book *Grid Systems* gives an overview of a selection of modernist grids, from Tschichold to the Bauhaus. Tracing paper overlays 'unpick' the nuances of some of these designs, which is an insightful and informative process. Shown on the opposite page is a grid for a poster by Odermatt & Tissi, that whilst being expressive, is built from a series of overlapping circles.

Exercise

1 Collect a series of posters, invitations and print materials.
2 Using tracing paper, overlay the designs and try to find the 'patterns' that underpin these designs.

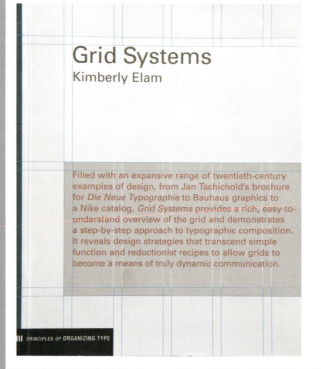

Kimberley Elam is chairperson of the Graphic and Interactive Communications Department at the Ringling College of Art and Design in Sarasota, Florida.
Her book contains examples of designers including Willi Kunz, Emil Ruder, Herbert Bayer, Siegfried Odermatt and Rosemarie Tissi, and Richard P. Lohse.

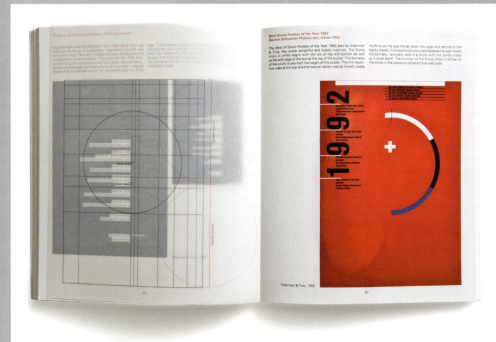

Aim

To encourage you to look at grids in a new way. The grid provides order, but it also underpins many contemporary and expressive forms. The grid can be found in many unlikely places, and beginning to explore a range of different approaches will help to inform and enrich your own design practice.

Outcome

A series of overlayed grid designs.

Suggested reading

- *Making and Breaking the Grid: A Layout Design Workshop* by Timothy Samara (Rockport Publishers, 2005)
- *Grid Index* by Carsten Nicolai (Die Gestalten Verlag, illustrated edition, 2009)

Industry view: Bedow | **Design activity: Looking at grids**

Client: University of the West of England

Design: Thirteen

Grid properties: Visible grid helps to structure page content

University of the West of England

This website was created by Thirteen for the University of the West of England, UK and features a visible grid that helps to structure the pages into clear divisions, enabling type and images to be placed in line with reading conventions typical to print media. This type of presentation lends the design a relevant and fresh feel. The colour block offers a clear navigation path and establishes a hierarchy, whilst the web pages make use of a graph paper background, referencing the academic nature of the organization.

Chapter 6
Online grids

Throughout this book, we have looked at how grids can be developed, used and implemented to great effect. Unlike printed items, where the designer has ultimate control over how a piece of work is presented, design online involves special considerations – as work will ultimately appear differently on different browsers and platforms.

Digital media gives designers the opportunity to make work feel relevant and fresh in a dynamic way that print simply can't. One of the first choices that a designer faces is whether to take advantage of the limitless space available on a digital page in both the vertical and horizontal orientations, or whether a fixed page format will work best. The lessons learnt from the printed page are still relevant to all online presentation, and are arguably more important than ever as designers strive to preserve the beauty of proportion and form in the online arena.

'The grid makes it possible to bring all the elements of design – type characters, photography, drawing and colour – into a formal relationship to each other; that is to say, the grid system is a means to introducing order into a design.'

Josef Müller-Brockmann

The online grid

Many of the basic principles of the grid can be translated directly from the page onto the screen. The grid is a means of ordering content and making a logical frame for a hierarchy of information.

Both on-page and on-screen there are recurrent themes, such as the position of items on a page, and their relationship to the edges or perimeter of it. Where we place items also starts to introduce a sense of hierarchy or structure into a design. The use of a grid, whether it is ultimately visible, or left as a background element, acts as a kind of 'scaffolding', making the placement of objects easier. In essence, the grid takes the element of chance out of a design, creating a sense of order out of intentional decision-making.

Marcus O'Reilly Architects (facing and following pages)
This website for an architecture practice creates a sense of calm and beauty through its restrained use of elements and white space. The vibrancy of the architectural photography becomes the emphasis, with the other grid-based elements fading into the background. A series of thumbnail images nestles below the main image area, creating a simple, intuitive navigation system.

Hierarchy
The arrangement of objects, images and text into an intended or logical order. Within design, hierarchy can be used to simplify a narrative or story, making the delivery of information more succinct and successful.

Client: Marcus O'Reilly
Architects
Design: Motherbird
Grid properties: Elegant grid
structure creates a sense of
space and emphasizes the
quality of the imagery

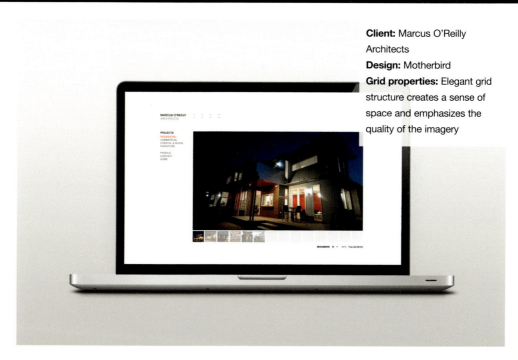

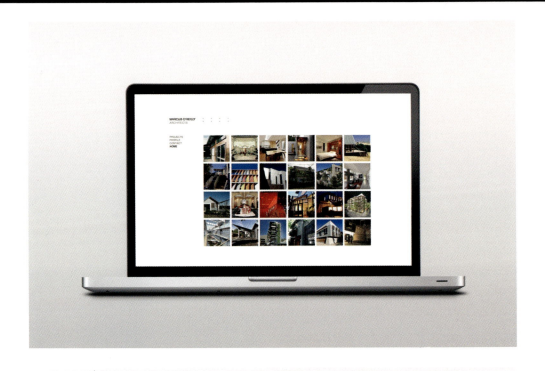

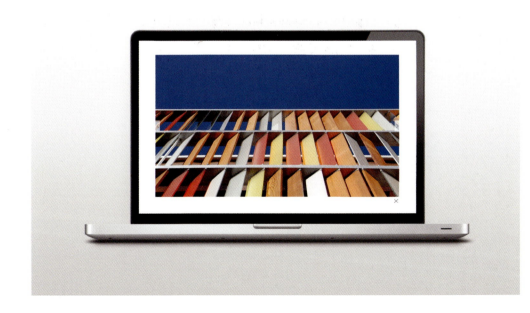

Formality versus informality
We often think of the grid, and particularly the online grid, as being somewhat formal or rigid. There are ways of breaking this convention, however, and of creating dynamic and interesting layouts that are still practical and logical to use.

Recent developments have seen the rise of easy-to-create content management systems (CMS) driven by open-source applications like WordPress. The advantage of these systems over traditional programming methods is that they require limited programming skills to update, or to contribute or add content to. This means that sites can be more active in their content, and changed at minimal cost. This slightly more informal approach can create sites that are far more engaging from the user's point of view. We want, and even demand, change and these CMS systems enable websites to have the same user-friendly operationality as blogs and social media.

The Cathedral Group (facing page)
This website for a building development (designed by Studio Myerscough, with programming by Twintoe) uses a WordPress engine to allow easy updating and content generation. The column structure makes use of a simple grid, in three vertical strips. This formality is then broken by the eclectic and ever-changing content on the site. The use of large imagery and limited text acts as a form of visual shorthand, working in a similar way to a newspaper, where readers 'skim' the images and headlines before deciding on what to read. This structure also negates the need for a traditional menu structure, minimizing buttons, click-throughs and other unnecessary visual 'noise'.

THE OLD VINYL FACTORY

Client: The Cathedral Group
Design: Studio Myerscough
Grid properties: Eclectic arrangement of elements creating an informal online grid

History of The Old Vinyl Factory

The Old Vinyl Factory

Wallis, Gilbert & Partners

Vinyl Canteen

The creative team

The developers

Vinyl Canteen: This week's menu

Space available to be let

The Old Vinyl Factory brochure

Record of the week

Tell us what you thi
Monday, March 19th, 2012

This week we are announcing some of our plans for the future of The Old Vinyl Factory. Come to The Shipping Building at the following times and let us know what you think:

Thursday 22nd March 6.00pm to 8.00pm
Saturday 24th March 10.00am to 4.00pm

Tick tock, Ken The Clock
Thursday, March 15th, 2012

Meet Ken Gilbert aka Ken the Clock. Ken used to maintain the clock on-site at The Old Vinyl Factory when it was the EMI and HMV's headquarters and 12,000 people worked in the surrounding factories. We invited some former EMI employees along to our PICTURE THIS exhibition in The Shipping Building to reminisce about the good old days. Ken particularly liked seeing the new bikes we have provided for the current employees on-site as when he worked at EMI everyone used to cycle to work. Meet more of the former EMI employees here. Read more

Phase II gets go ahead from Hillingdon Council
Wednesday, February 15th, 2012

Last night the London Borough of Hillingdon's planning committee unanimously passed a resolution to grant planning consent for phase two of our regeneration at The Old Vinyl Factory. The Gatefold Building will provide 132 new apartments, a community café and business incubator units. It's a big step on the road to the complete redevelopment of a site that will bring major investment and wider benefits to Hayes.

Sound recording…
Tuesday, November 22nd, 2011

This is our new sound booth in the Shipping Building. Part meeting room, part performance space, it's available to community groups who might want to use it. Seats 8 round a table and about 30 in theatre style seating. Contact Catherine Dixon here if you want to find out more.

We built this city…
Tuesday, November 22nd, 2011

New graphics up in the Vinyl Canteen, designed by Morag Myerscough. Hayes truly was built on Rock n Roll - we continue the vibe…

Web basics – fixed or flexible?

Arguably the biggest variant in website design is whether the site is fixed, or whether it is flexible. There is no absolute rule as to which is more appropriate, though most commercial and mass-market sites tend to be flexible.

Fixed width

Fixed-width pages have widths that do not change, regardless of browser size. This is achieved by using specific pixel numbers (absolute measurements) for the widths of page divisions. This system can be used when you need a design to look exactly the same on any browser, no matter how wide or narrow it is. However, this method does not take into account the viewers of the information. People who have browsers that are narrower than the design will have to scroll horizontally in order to see everything, while people with extremely wide browsers will have large amounts of empty space on their screens.

Flexible width

Flexible-width pages vary depending on how wide the user's browser window is. They can be achieved by using percentages or relative measurements of the widths of page divisions. Flexible width allows a designer to create pages that change to accommodate screen width.

Client: 3 Deep

Design: 3 Deep

Grid properties: Site with main information panel, and gridded sub-menu

3 DEEP

OUR DNA   OUR PROCESS   OUR PROJECTS   OUR DEPARTMENTS   OUR WORLD   OUR V

WE CREATE EXTRAORDINARY BRANDS FOR EXTRAORDINARY PEOPLE

CLICK HERE TO LEARN MORE

OUR DNA

For more than 15 years we have been creating extraordinary brands for extraordinary people. Discover what makes us tick.
Learn more

OUR PROCESS

Discover how we deliver commercial results through innovative creative thinking.
Learn more

OUR PROJECTS

Whilst our work is creative, our success is measured in numbers. Discover why our work makes commercial sense.
Learn more

OUR DEPARTMENTS

Reaching consumers is the responsibility of many, not just a few. Discover how our departments can help.
Learn more

OUR WORLD

Any community has its custodians, influencers and guardians. Discover those who influence and inform our world.
Learn more

OUR VOICE

Immerse yourself in our world of extraordinary brands, compelling ideas and inspirational people.
Learn more

CONTACT

If you are looking to create value and build demand for your brand, we would love to hear from you.
Learn more

SUBSCRIBE

Subscribe to our enews for regular inspiration, updates and special offers.
Learn more

3 Deep

3 Deep's website features a layout in which there is a central key panel, and then a gridded sub-menu below. This layout is editorial in construction and delivery – being reminiscent of a newspaper (through the use of Scotch Rules and rigid columns) while embracing the benefits of online technology. The site has a clear sense of hierarchy and order, while still being engaging and dynamic.

Translating the grid to the screen
Organizations have a presence both in print and online. Grids can therefore prove a useful tool for translating design style from one media to another.

Graphic elements can be translated, but equally the approach to a grid or structure can also form an important part of an overall identity. This could include the relationship to the edge of the page or the use of background patterns, as the example on this page demonstrates.

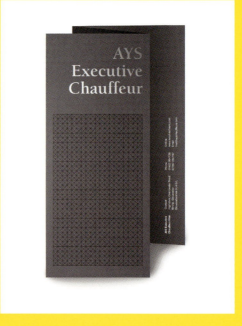

AYS Executive Chauffeur

In the printed form of this identity, the logotype and graphic patterns are formed using foils and spot varnishes. In an online environment, you can't use the same printing effects, but consistency can still be created. The pattern on the front of the brochure becomes a background pattern, a liquid, expandable element on the website. Other elements have to be adapted; text that runs vertically on printed items, for instance, can't be mimicked online. The key to the success of a brand working across multiple media is to embrace the advantages of each.

Client: AYS Executive Chauffeur

Design: Lost & Found Creative

Grid properties: Grid and pattern translated from print to screen

Orientation

One of the key differences between the digital and print environments is the page size that can be used. While a print job may be limited by the size of the paper stock and printing machines available, a digital page can have any dimension and be formed to fit the content perfectly.

The grid on a digital page can extend vertically and horizontally as far as it needs to, with subsequent pages each having a different size. On the other hand, a print publication tends to have pages of the same size. For example, a website could have a full-size page of a man standing up in portrait format with the next page having the same man lying down in landscape format, with each page having the dimensions needed to completely show the subject. Due to the specific restrictions inherent to digital formats, it is less common to see the use of angular text or broadside formats.

Horizontal

Horizontal orientation is suitable for a landscape presentation that scrolls left and right. This is evident in the example opposite, which allows a viewer to pan around a room. This orientation conveys the possibility of having many columns side by side. It also presents a wide potential grid, which can be scrolled horizontally.

Vertical

Vertical orientation is suitable for a portrait presentation that scrolls up and down, allowing a viewer to descend down a body of information. This offers the possibility of having a limited amount of very long columns, similar to a traditional editorial grid.

Descending

A descending orientation sees layers of design elements and content building upon one another, eventually reaching the final look of the design.

Client: UTOUP

Design: UTOUP

Grid properties: Horizontal 'slivers' of project images create an eclectic pattern

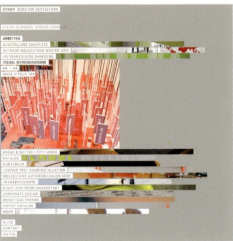

Translating the grid to the screen | **Orientation** | Industry view: Morse Studio

UTOUP

This website for German design group UTOUP uses a series of horizontal image slivers or windows to generate a sense of intrigue. The juxtaposition of the images hints at the work below. Once expanded, the showcased work reads as a series of horizontally scrolling images.

Siobhan Davies Dance

This website for Siobhan Davies Dance uses a vertical structure to create order and add a dynamic element, reflecting the nature of the site. The main 'landing' page uses a simple three-column structure (above) to direct viewers to the appropriate part of the site. Once in a sub-section, as shown on the facing page, the vertical theme is used to create a sense of playful pace, with images and text placement reflecting the theme of dance.

SIOBHAN DAVIES DANCE

One of the UK's leading dance companies Siobhan Davies Dance develops and presents the distinctive choreographic voice of its founder and director.

> Home
> Siobhan Davies Dance works
> Projects for schools & young people
> Side by Side
> News

SIOBHAN DAVIES STUDIOS

Siobhan Davies Studios host a rich mix of events, classes, workshops and exhibitions designed to stimulate both the mind and the body.

> Home
> Events and exhibitions
> Dance classes
> Complementary therapies
> News

SIOBHAN DAVIES RELAY

Client: Siobhan Davies Dance
Design: Bullet Creative
Grid properties: Vertical strips containing images and text create a dynamic, yet structured website

Siobhan Davies Relay broadcasts digital exchanges of ideas about dance and choreography, including the recently launched Siobhan Davies Replay.

> Home
> Siobhan Davies Replay
> Conversations on Making
> Parallel Voices 2010
> Exhibitions archive

SIOBHAN DAVIES STUDIOS

Home
Classes
Therapies
Events & Exhibitions
Space Hire
About

News
Contact
Mailing List
Siobhan Davies Dance
Siobhan Davies Relay

Graham Gussin and David Chipperfield in conversation >

See our new programme of events and exhibitions including the 60|40 Starting Point Series >

Footfall - traipse, meander, tiptoe or strut to Siobhan Davies Studios on 15 July >

Welcome to a unique space for dance in London. "These studios will make a real difference and it is my intention that they should benefit dancers, choreographers and other artists by being a beautiful place to work."
Siobhan Davies

Search   Go

Siobhan Davies Studios · Siobhan Davies Dance· Siobhan Davies Relay
85 St George's Road, London, SE1 6ER · 020 7091 9650

Mailing list   Join

Translating the grid to the screen | **Orientation** | Industry view: Morse Studio

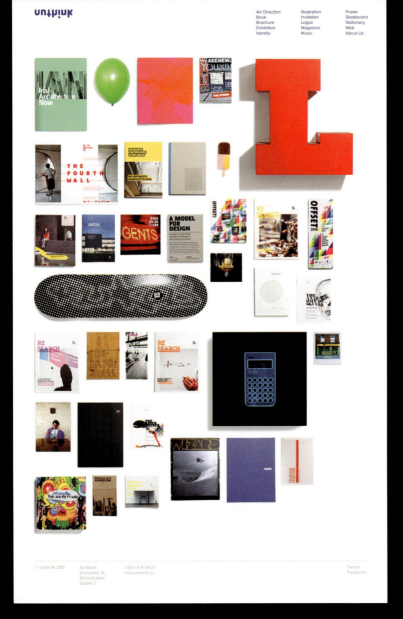

Unthink

Unthink's website uses a vertically oriented format to showcase their work. The grid on the homepage creates a montage of eclectic elements, leading through to expanded pages of project images and text.

Art Direction
Book
Brochure
Exhibition
Identity

Illustration
Invitation
Logos
Magazine
Music

Poster
Skateboard
Stationery
Web
About Us

A Space For Learning

Irish Architecture Foundation / Exhibition / Identity

A project which teamed up architects with transition year students to examine how schools could be improved and culminated in an exhibition in the NCAD Gallery. The bespoke typeface we created for the accompanying book was used on exhibition signage. Bold window graphics created awareness on the street and inside printed cardboard boxes held info about the exhibits.

Share This on Facebook / Twitter

A SPACE FOR LEARNING

Industry view: Morse Studio

This case study shows the identity, print and web designs for architecture practice, Lyn Atelier. The solution uses a set of design principles and elements across a range of media and applications.

Lyn Atelier is an architecture and design practice who commissioned Morse Studio to create a distinctive, but unobtrusive identity to reflect the values of the practice. The resulting design solution is a series of thin rules that work across all media. Was it always considered from the start that this identity would need to work across multiple applications and platforms?

Our brief was to produce a visual identity for Lyn that works in both print and online applications. As with all of our branding solutions, we are as interested in the behaviour of the assets with one another as we are in the primary mark itself. Our solution for Lyn originates from the idea of evident process – embracing the underlying structure and utilizing it as a visual device. Although very structural, the logotype and set of rules are very flexible and adaptable across various applications.

Orientation | **Industry view: Morse Studio** | Design activity: Translation on to the screen

Can you describe the freedoms or limitations you feel exist in working across several media? In this project, you have achieved delicacy in both print and on-screen. Can you elaborate on this process?
Aside from the given differences between the two mediums, we don't tend to treat online and print much differently; the same formal considerations exist for both. Whether on-screen or in print, it is important that the expression of the visual assets remains coherent.

Achieving consistent delicacy throughout required optical adjustments both online and in print; from the tone of the website background and pixel interpolation of the thin rules, to the optical adjustments required to balance horizontal rules with verticals.

Morse Studio is a London-based design agency working across different media for a wide range of clients. Their work is underpinned by a purity of execution and an ability to create simple, yet engaging solutions.
www.morsestudio.com

Translating elements on to screen requires careful consideration. Formal elements, divisions of space and placement of text and image must work together to create a harmonious design.

Orientation | **Industry view: Morse Studio** | Design activity: Translation on to the screen

Design activity:
Translation on to the screen

Premise

Josef Müller-Brockmann was a Swiss graphic designer and teacher who established a design studio in Zurich in the early 1930s. Later appointed design consultant to IBM, Brockmann's work followed in the tradition of Swiss modernist design, such as that of Jan Tschichold and the Russian constructivists, including El Lissitzky. His seminal book, *Grid Systems in Graphic Design* (1981), proposes a central principle – that the grid is a controlling element that can be applied to all aspects of design. Brockmann's earlier book, *The Graphic Artist and his Design Problems* (1961), is recognized as one of the first publications to use the grid as a universal design tool.

Beginning with an exploration of how different elements have an influence on a design, for example different typefaces and degrees of leading, the book progresses to demonstrate how complex grids can be developed for a multitude of different purposes.

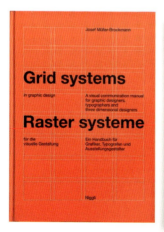
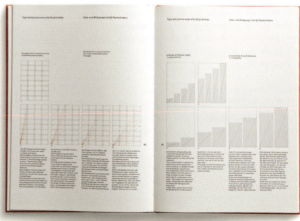

Exercise

1 Take an A4 piece of paper and design a series of different grids, for example a 2-, 3-, 4- or 5-column grid.
2 Populate these grids with text (this can be dummy or 'Greek' text) and observe how the readability of the text is affected. You will notice that some typefaces have varying 'set-widths', meaning that some typefaces are wider than others, even when set at the same point size (see below). When you alter a typeface, you may also need to alter the grid.

Aim

To understand that the grid has a relationship to the elements that it contains – if you change one, you may need to change the other.

Outcome

A series of experiments looking at the relationship between the grid and typefaces of varying set-widths.

Suggested reading

* *Swiss Graphic Design: The Origins and Growth of an International Style 1920–1965,* Richard Hollis (Laurence King, new edition, 2006)

Different set widths

Different set widths

Two typefaces set at the same point size occupy different amounts of space. This means that they will behave differently if set in the same grid. One will have more characters per line than the other, and ultimately this relationship is symbiotic: if you alter one element, you may also need to consider altering another.

A-series paper sizes
ISO metric standard paper size based on the square root of two ratio. The A0 sheet (841 x 1,189mm/33.1 x 46.8 in) is one square metre and each size (A1, A2, A3, A4, etc.) differs from the next by a factor of either 2 or 0.5.

Active page area
An area on the page that attracts the eye.

Alignment
Text location within a text block in the vertical and horizontal planes.

Anatomy of a page
The different structures that organize and present information on a page.

Angular grid
A grid where text and image elements are used at an angle.

Asymmetrical grid
A grid that is the same on recto and verso pages, which typically introduces a bias towards one side of the page (usually the left).

Axis
The invisible line of balance or stress that runs through a design.

B-series paper sizes
ISO metric standard paper size based on the square root of two ratio. B-sizes are intermediate sizes to the A-series sizes.

Baseline grid
A graphic foundation composed of lines on which a design is constructed.

Binding
Any of several processes that holds together the pages or sections of a publication using stitches, wire, glue or other medium.

Body copy
Text that forms the main part of a work.

Broadside
Text presented to read vertically rather than horizontally.

Captions
Text that describes or names graphic elements.

Column
A vertical area or field into which text is flowed.

Composition
The combination of text and image elements to create a design.

Compound grid
A grid combining columns and modules.

Cross-alignment
A typographical hierarchy where the different levels share a common relationship, and can be aligned in the same grid.

F-shaped reading pattern
A reading pattern produced by attempting to quickly draw information from a website.

Fibonacci numbers
A series of numbers discovered by Fibonacci where each number is the sum of the preceding two. They are important because of their link to the 8:13 ratio, also known as the golden section.

Fold (web page)
An imaginary line signifying the limit of what can be seen on a Web page before having to scroll down.

Folios
Page numbers.

Format
The size/proportions of a book or page. This includes the print finishing and binding of the piece.

Grouping
Bringing together or gathering units or blocks of related information.

Gutter
The space that comprises the fore-edge or outer edge of a page, which is parallel to the back and the trim. It is the centre alleyway where two pages meet at the spine. It could also mean the space between text columns.

Head margin
The space at the top of the page; also called top margin.

Hierarchy
A logical, organized and visual guide for text headings, indicating levels of importance.

Horizontal alignment
The lining up of text in a field, on its horizontal plane. Text can be aligned centre, range right, range left, or justified.

Hyphenation
The insertion of a hyphen at the point where a word is broken in a justified text block.

Image
A visual element (e.g. photograph, diagram, drawing).

Intensity
Refers to how crowded a design or spread is.

International Paper Sizes
A range of standard metric paper sizes developed by the ISO.

Inverted pyramid
A style of presenting information in which the most important information leads a piece, followed by further information decreasing in importance.

Justified
Text that is extended across the measure, aligning on both left and right margins.

Juxtaposition
The placement of different elements side by side in order to establish links or emphasize contrast.

Layout
The placement of text and images to give the general appearance of the printed page.

Letter spacing
The distance between the letters of a word.

Locking to a grid
Fixing text to the baseline grid so that the grid determines spacing between text lines.

Marginalia
Text matter that appears in the page margins.

Margins
The spaces surrounding a text block at the sides, top and bottom of a page.

Measure
The width, in characters, of a page or text column.

Module-based grid
A grid composed of an array of modules or fields, usually squares.

Orientation
The plane or direction in which text and images are used.

Pagination
The arrangement and numbering of pages in a publication.

Passepartout
A frame or border around an image or other element.

Passive page area
An area of a page that does not attract the eye.

Perimeter
The outer edge of a page or spread.

Proportion
The scale relationship between page elements.

Rule of odds
A composition guide stipulating that an odd number of elements is more interesting than an even number.

Rule of thirds
A composition guide using a 3 x 3 grid to create active hotspots.

Symmetrical grid
A grid where the recto and verso pages mirror each other.

Typographic colour
Colour blocks created by text elements as a result of font, weight and size.

Vertical alignment
Where type or text is aligned on a vertical plane within a field. Text can be arranged to align from the top, the bottom, the centre, or be justified within the text block.

White space
The unused space between design elements.

Glossary | Index

3 Deep 102, 103, 181

A
absolute measurements 36
active juxtaposition 44
active page areas 12
active perimeter 134
anatomy of a page 34–36
Andy Vella 159
angular arrangement 41
angular grids 84–85
asymmetrical grids 70–71, 72
axis 138–141
axis orientated 41

B
baseline 98–99, 100
Bedow 7, 166–169
Bedow, Perniclas 166
Birdsall, Derek 144
Bringhurst, Robert 124
broadside orientation 41, 82–83
Bullet Creative 187

C
caption-oriented grids 152–153
Cienfuegos, Alberto 26
column widths 112–115
columns 93, 106–115
combinations 74–75
content management systems
        (CMS) 178

D
Danko, Tegan 21
Dawson, Peter 8, 21, 120, 122
design, function of 20–25
design activities
        grid and identity 30
        listen to the pigeons 90
        looking at grids 170
        looking at space 62
        translation on to screen
                194
        typographic style 124
diagonal grids 84–85
Disciplina 139
display type 95
drawing grids 50–53

E
Eckersley, Richard 157
Elam, Kimberley 170
Elovsson, Thomas 166
environmental grids 148–151
expression, grid as 156–159
eye-tracking (reading pages)
        12–15, 16, 152

F
F-pattern, reading 16
Faydherbe/De Vringer 32, 57,
        79, 80, 135, 136
Fibonacci numbers 51
fixed-width pages 180–181
flexible-width pages 180–181
floating plates 163
fold 16
folios 116–119
form and function 20–25
formality 178
Froshaug, Anthony 33
function of design 20–25
function of grids 9–10

G
Gabor Palotai Design 3, 86–89,
        149, 161
Gerstner, Karl 52
Gill, Bob 90
Grade Design 8, 21, 39, 73,
        120–123
graphic identity 148, 160–165
grouping elements 40

H
hanging line 100
hierarchy 46–49, 174
Hofmann, Armin 62
horizontal alignment 104
horizontal movement 40, 76–77
hotspots 46
Hurlburt, Allen 93

I
identity, graphic 148, 160–165
images 37, 100–103
industry views
        Bedow 166–169
        Gabor Palotai Design
                86–89
        Grade Design 120–123
        Lavernia & Cienfuegos
                Diseño 26–29
        Morse Studio 190–193
        Z3/Studio 58–61
informality 178
information, organizing 10

J
juxtaposition 44, 142–143

K
Kape, James 43
kerning 97
Knowles, Jeff 162

L
Lavernia, Nacho 26
Lavernia & Cienfugeos Diseño
        26–29
letter spacing 97
Lost & Found Creative 183
Lupton, Ellen 127

M
marginalia 68
measurements 36–37
Michael Harvey 143
modernism 20, 38
modules 72–73
Morse Studio 190–193
Motherbird 175
Mousegraphics 45
Müller-Brockmann, Josef 10,
        65, 173, 194

N
narrative 130
NB: Studio 64, 110, 129
negative leading 98

O
odds, rule of 56–57
Ömse 42–43
online grids 173, 174–177
        web pages 16, 180–181
organizing information 10
orientation 184–189
        broadside 41, 82–83
overview of grids 6
        basic framework 33
        elements 93
        grid usage 127
        need for 9
        online grids 173
        types 65

P
pages
        anatomy of 34–36
        dynamics 44
        reading 12–15, 16, 152
        shapes on 38–43
        web pages 16, 180–181
Palmer-Edwards, Paul 122
passepartout 41, 137
passive juxtaposition 44
passive page areas 12
passive perimeter 134
Pentagram 15, 95, 97, 137, 145
perimeter 40, 134–137
pivots, visual 78
principles, grids 10
proportion 44–45
pull quotes 153

Q
quantitative information grids
      154–155
quotes, pull 153

R
Rand, Paul 9
reading pages 12–15, 16, 152
relative measurements 36
Research Studios 14, 47, 92,
      111, 162
rivers 105
rule of odds 56–57
rule of thirds 54–55
runaround feature 101

S
scale 130–133
scanning pages 12–15, 152
scholar's margin 95
screens, viewing 16–19
SEA Design 131
set solid 98
shapes on pages 38–43
Smith, Briton 43
Social Design 75, 113
Studio Myerscough 179
Studio Output 17
Sullivan, Louis 20
symmetrical grids 66–69, 72

T
tapestry 137
text block 95
Third Eye Design
      anatomy of pages 35
      angular grids 85
      columns 107, 115
      folios 118, 119
      horizontal movement 77
      rule of thirds 55
      vertical movement 81
thirds, rule of 54–55
Thirteen 67, 83, 153, 155, 172
thumbnails 68
translating grids to screen
      182–183
translation plates 163
Tschichold, Jan 30–31, 50
type 37, 94–97, 112–115
type widths 112–115
typographic colour 96

U
Unthink 49, 147, 189
UTOUP 11, 185

V
Vast Agency, The 48
vertical alignment 105
vertical movement 40, 78–81
visible grids 128–129
visual pivots 78
Voice Design 114

W
web pages 16, 180–181
Webb, James 132
Webb & Webb Design 13, 24,
      25, 126, 132
white space 144–147
why not associates 109
word spacing 97

X
x-height 98

Z
Z3/Studio 58–61

Agency	Contact	Page number
3 Deep	www.3deep.com.au	102–3, 181
Andy Vella	www.velladesign.com	158–9
Bedow	www.bedow.se	7, 166–9
Bullet Creative	www.bulletcreative.com	186–7
Disciplina	www.cargocollective.com/disciplina	139–141
Faydherbe/De Vringer	www.ben-wout.nl	32, 57, 78–9, 80, 134–7, 138
Gabor Palotai Design	www.gaborpalotai.com	3, 86–9, 148–151, 160–1
Grade Design	www.gradedesign.com	8, 21, 39, 73,
Lavernia & Cienfuegos Diseño	www.lavernia–cienfuegos.com	27–9
Lost & Found Creative	www.lostandfoundcreative.co.uk	182–3
Michael Harvey	www.michaelharveyphoto.com	143
Mousegraphics	www. www.mousegraphics.gr	45
Morse Studio	www.morsestudio.com	190–3
Motherbird	www.motherbird.com.au	174–7
NB: Studio	www.nbstudio.co.uk	64–5, 110–1, 128–9
Ömse	www.omsestudio.com	42–3
Pentagram	www.pentagram.com	15, 95, 97, 137, 145
Research Studios	www.researchstudios.com	14, 47, 92–3, 111, 162–5
Richard Eckersley	www.richardeckersley.net	156–7
SEA Design	www.seadesign.co.uk	131
Social Design	www.socialuk.com	75, 113
Studio Myerscough	www.studiomyerscough.co.uk	178–9
Studio Output	www.studio-output.com	16–19
The Vast Agency	www.thevastagency.com	48
Third Eye Design	www.thirdeyedesign.co.uk	35, 55, 76–7, 80–1, 85, 106–7, 115, 118–9, 120–3
Thirteen	www.thirteen.co.uk	67, 83, 153, 155, 172
Unthink	www.unthink.ie	49, 146–7, 188–9
UTOUP	www.utoup.com	11, 185
Voice Design	www.voicedesign.net	114
Webb & Webb	www.webbandwebb.co.uk	12–13, 24–5, 126–7, 132–3
why not associates	www.whynotassociates.com	109
Z3/Studio	www.designbyz3.com	58–61

All reasonable attempts have been made to trace, clear and credit the copyright holders of the images reproduced in this book. However, if any credits have been inadvertently omitted, the publisher will endeavour to incorporate amendments in future editions.

Lost and Found Creative©Andrew Hussey, Creative Director, Lost and Found Creative; Morse©Morse Studio Ltd.; Grade©Grade Design Consultants Limited; Bedow©Bedow; 3 Deep©3 Deep 2012; Studio Myerscough©Studio Myerscough; Disciplina©2011 Disciplina; Vella Design©Andy Vella/Foruli; UTOUP©UTOUP; Gabor Palotai Design©Gabor Palotai Design.

We would like to thank everyone who supported us during the project – the many art directors, designers and creatives who showed great generosity in allowing us to reproduce their work. Thanks to Xavier Young for his patience, determination and skill in photographing the work showcased. And a final big thanks to Brian Morris, Colette Meacher and all the staff at AVA Publishing.

Publisher's note

The subject of ethics is not new, yet its consideration within the applied visual arts is perhaps not as prevalent as it might be. Our aim here is to help a new generation of students, educators and practitioners find a methodology for structuring their thoughts and reflections in this vital area.

AVA Publishing hopes that these **Working with ethics** pages provide a platform for consideration and a flexible method for incorporating ethical concerns in the work of educators, students and professionals. Our approach consists of four parts:

The **introduction** is intended to be an accessible snapshot of the ethical landscape, both in terms of historical development and current dominant themes.

The **framework** positions ethical consideration into four areas and poses questions about the practical implications that might occur. Marking your response to each of these questions on the scale shown will allow your reactions to be further explored by comparison.

The **case study** sets out a real project and then poses some ethical questions for further consideration. This is a focus point for a debate rather than a critical analysis so there are no predetermined right or wrong answers.

A selection of **further reading** for you to consider areas of particular interest in more detail.

Ethical: aware-ness/ reflect-ion/ debate

Working with ethics

Ethics is a complex subject that interlaces the idea of responsibilities to society with a wide range of considerations relevant to the character and happiness of the individual. It concerns virtues of compassion, loyalty and strength, but also of confidence, imagination, humour and optimism. As introduced in ancient Greek philosophy, the fundamental ethical question is: *what should I do?* How we might pursue a 'good' life not only raises moral concerns about the effects of our actions on others, but also personal concerns about our own integrity.

In modern times the most important and controversial questions in ethics have been the moral ones. With growing populations and improvements in mobility and communications, it is not surprising that considerations about how to structure our lives together on the planet should come to the forefront. For visual artists and communicators, it should be no surprise that these considerations will enter into the creative process.

Some ethical considerations are already enshrined in government laws and regulations or in professional codes of conduct. For example, plagiarism and breaches of confidentiality can be punishable offences. Legislation in various nations makes it unlawful to exclude people with disabilities from accessing information or spaces. The trade of ivory as a material has been banned in many countries. In these cases, a clear line has been drawn under what is unacceptable.

But most ethical matters remain open to debate, among experts and lay-people alike, and in the end we have to make our own choices on the basis of our own guiding principles or values. Is it more ethical to work for a charity than for a commercial company? Is it unethical to create something that others find ugly or offensive?

Specific questions such as these may lead to other questions that are more abstract. For example, is it only effects on humans (and what they care about) that are important, or might effects on the natural world require attention too?

Is promoting ethical consequences justified even when it requires ethical sacrifices along the way? Must there be a single unifying theory of ethics (such as the Utilitarian thesis that the right course of action is always the one that leads to the greatest happiness of the greatest number), or might there always be many different ethical values that pull a person in various directions?

As we enter into ethical debate and engage with these dilemmas on a personal and professional level, we may change our views or change our view of others. The real test though is whether, as we reflect on these matters, we change the way we act as well as the way we think. Socrates, the 'father' of philosophy, proposed that people will naturally do 'good' if they know what is right. But this point might only lead us to yet another question: *how do we know what is right?*

You

What are your ethical beliefs?

Central to everything you do will be your attitude to people and issues around you. For some people, their ethics are an active part of the decisions they make every day as a consumer, a voter or a working professional. Others may think about ethics very little and yet this does not automatically make them unethical. Personal beliefs, lifestyle, politics, nationality, religion, gender, class or education can all influence your ethical viewpoint.

Using the scale, where would you place yourself? What do you take into account to make your decision? Compare results with your friends or colleagues.

Your client

What are your terms?

Working relationships are central to whether ethics can be embedded into a project, and your conduct on a day-to-day basis is a demonstration of your professional ethics. The decision with the biggest impact is whom you choose to work with in the first place. Cigarette companies or arms traders are often-cited examples when talking about where a line might be drawn, but rarely are real situations so extreme. At what point might you turn down a project on ethical grounds and how much does the reality of having to earn a living affect your ability to choose?

Using the scale, where would you place a project? How does this compare to your personal ethical level?

01 02 03 04 05 06 07 08 09 10

01 02 03 04 05 06 07 08 09 10

Your specifications

What are the impacts of your materials?

In relatively recent times, we are learning that many natural materials are in short supply. At the same time, we are increasingly aware that some man-made materials can have harmful, long-term effects on people or the planet. How much do you know about the materials that you use? Do you know where they come from, how far they travel and under what conditions they are obtained? When your creation is no longer needed, will it be easy and safe to recycle? Will it disappear without a trace? Are these considerations your responsibility or are they out of your hands?

Using the scale, mark how ethical your material choices are.

Your creation

What is the purpose of your work?

Between you, your colleagues and an agreed brief, what will your creation achieve? What purpose will it have in society and will it make a positive contribution? Should your work result in more than commercial success or industry awards? Might your creation help save lives, educate, protect or inspire? Form and function are two established aspects of judging a creation, but there is little consensus on the obligations of visual artists and communicators toward society, or the role they might have in solving social or environmental problems. If you want recognition for being the creator, how responsible are you for what you create and where might that responsibility end?

Using the scale, mark how ethical the purpose of your work is.

01 02 03 04 05 06 07 08 09 10

01 02 03 04 05 06 07 08 09 10

Working with ethics

One aspect of graphic design that raises an ethical dilemma is that of its relationship with the creation of printed materials and the environmental impacts of print production. For example, in the UK, it is estimated that around 5.4 billion items of addressed direct mail are sent out every year and these, along with other promotional inserts, amount to over half a million tonnes of paper annually (almost 5 per cent of the UK consumption of paper and board). Response rates to mail campaigns are known to be between 1–3 per cent, making junk mail arguably one of the least environmentally friendly forms of print communication. As well as the use of paper or board, the design decisions to use scratch-off panels, heavily coated gloss finishes, full-colour ink-intensive graphics or glues for seals or fixings make paper more difficult to recycle once it has been discarded. How much responsibility should a graphic designer have in this situation if a client has already chosen to embark on a direct mail campaign and has a format in mind? Even if designers wish to minimise the environmental impacts of print materials, what might they most usefully do?

In 1951, Leo Burnett (the famous advertising executive known for creating the Jolly Green Giant and the Marlboro Man) was hired to create a campaign for Kellogg's new cereal, Sugar Frosted Flakes (now Frosties in the UK and Frosted Flakes in the US). Tony the Tiger, designed by children's book illustrator Martin Provensen, was one of four characters selected to sell the cereal. Newt the Gnu and Elmo the Elephant never made it to the shelves and after Tony proved more popular than Katy the Kangaroo, she was dropped from packs after the first year.

Whilst the orange-and-black tiger stripes and the red kerchief have remained, Provensen's original design for Tony has changed significantly since he first appeared in 1952. Tony started out with an American football-shaped head, which later became more rounded, and his eye colour changed from green to gold. Today, his head is more angular and he sits on a predominantly blue background. Tony was initially presented as a character that walked on all fours and was no bigger than a cereal box. By the 1970s, Tony's physique had developed into a slim and muscular six-foot-tall standing figure.

Between 1952 and 1995 Kellogg's are said to have spent more than USD$1 billion promoting Frosted Flakes with Tony's image, while generating USD$5.3 billion in gross US sales. But surveys by consumer rights groups such as Which? find that over 75 per cent of people believe that using characters on packaging makes it hard for parents to say no to their children. In these surveys, Kellogg's come under specific scrutiny for Frosties, which are said to contain one third sugar and more salt than the Food Standards Agency recommends. In response, Kellogg's have said: 'We are committed to responsibly marketing our brands and communicating their intrinsic qualities so that our customers can make informed choices.'

Food campaigners claim that the use of cartoon characters is a particularly manipulative part of the problem and governments should stop them being used on less healthy children's foods. But in 2008, spokespeople for the Food and Drink Federation in the UK, said: 'We are baffled as to why Which? wants to take all the fun out of food by banning popular brand characters, many of whom have been adding colour to supermarket shelves for more than 80 years.'

Is it more ethical to create promotional graphics for 'healthy' rather than 'unhealthy' food products?

Is it unethical to design cartoon characters to appeal to children for commercial purposes?

Would you have worked on this project, either now or in the 1950s?

I studied graphic design in Germany, and my professor emphasised the responsibility that designers and illustrators have towards the people they create things for.

Eric Carle
(illustrator)

Further reading

AIGA
Design Business and Ethics
2007, AIGA

Eaton, Marcia Muelder
Aesthetics and the Good Life
1989, Associated University Press

Ellison, David
Ethics and Aesthetics in European Modernist Literature:
From the Sublime to the Uncanny
2001, Cambridge University Press

Fenner, David E W (Ed)
Ethics and the Arts:
An Anthology
1995, Garland Reference Library of Social Science

Gini, Al and Marcoux, Alexei M
Case Studies in Business Ethics
2005, Prentice Hall

McDonough, William and Braungart, Michael
Cradle to Cradle:
Remaking the Way We Make Things
2002, North Point Press

Papanek, Victor
Design for the Real World:
Making to Measure
1972, Thames & Hudson

United Nations Global Compact
The Ten Principles
www.unglobalcompact.org/AboutTheGC/TheTenPrinciples/index.html